WORK-INS, SIT-INS AND INDUSTRIAL DEMOCRACY

Work-ins, Sit-ins and Industrial Democracy

The Implications of Factory Occupations in Great Britain in the Early 'Seventies

by Ken Coates

Spokesman

First published in 1981 by:
Spokesman
Bertrand Russell House
Gamble Street
Nottingham

Copyright © Ken Coates 1981

This book is copyright under the Berne Convention. All rights are reserved. Apart from any fair dealing for the purpose of private study, research, criticism or review, as permitted under the Copyright Act, 1956, no part of this publication may be reproduced stored in a retrieval system, or transmitted, in any form or by any means, electronic, electrical, chemical, mechanical, photocopying, recording or otherwise, without the prior permission of the copyright owner. Enquiries should be addressed to the publishers.

British Library Cataloguing in Publication Data:
Coates, Ken
Work-ins, sit-ins and industrial democracy
1. Sit-down strikes — Great Britain
2. Unemployed — Great Britain
1. Title
331.89'26 HD5165.A6.
Cloth ISBN 0 85124 278 2
Paper ISBN 0 85124 277 4

Printed by the Russell Press Ltd., Nottingham

*For my daughter
Tali*

Contents

I	Factory Occupations	11
II	UCS: A Lame Duck Takes Wing	21
III	Some Lessons	39
IV	Sit-ins	49
V	Working on in Sheffield: A Steel Man's Account	75
VI	The Social Audit	83
VII	Spreading out all over . . .	101
VIII	The TUC takes its stand	123
IX	A Rebirth of Co-operation?	133
X	A Conclusion and a New Beginning	149
	Bibliography	167
	Index	171

Glossary of Acronyms

ACTT	Association of Cinematograph, Television and Allied Technicians
APEX	Association of Professional, Executive, Clerical and Computer Staff
ASTMS	Association of Scientific, Technical and Managerial Staffs
AUEW	Amalgamated Union of Engineering Workers
BMC	British Motor Corporation
CEU	Constructional Engineers' Union
DATA	Draughtsmen & Allied Technicians' Association (subsequently known as TASS)
EAO	European Automotive Operations (Fords')
EEPTU	Electrical, Electronic, Telecommunications and Plumbing Union
GEC	General Electric Company
GMWU	General and Municipal Workers' Union
ICI	Imperial Chemical Industries
ICOM	Industrial Common Ownership Movement
IPD	International Property Development
KME	Kirkby Manufacturing and Engineering Company
MSC	Manpower Services Commission
NATKE	National Association of Theatrical, Television and Kine Employees
NATSOPA	National Society of Operative Printers, Graphical and Media Personnel
NGA	National Graphical Association
NUFLAT	National Union of Footwear, Leather and Allied Trades
NUFTO	National Union of Footwear Trades Operatives
NUJ	National Union of Journalists
NUPE	National Union of Public Employees
PLP	Parliamentary Labour Party
SIB	Shipbuilding Industry Board
SLADE	Society of Lithographic Artists, Designers, Engravers and Process Workers
SOGAT	Society of Graphical and Allied Trades
TASS	Technical, Administrative, Supervisory Section (of the Engineers' Union)
T&GWU	Transport and General Workers' Union
UCATT	Union of Construction Allied Trades and Technicians
UCS	Upper Clyde Shipbuilders

Introduction

This book contains an account of the movement of factory occupations, "work-ins" and "sit-ins" which spread from the Glasgow shipyards out through many other factories and workshops in the first half of the 'seventies.

Nearly all of it was written at the time, but its publication was delayed, partly because of technical publishing difficulties, and partly because it had to be set aside when I was run over and put out of action for a while. I was persuaded to return to the manuscript, with all its inadequacies, because parts of it had already been circulated and used, and there were insistent requests from various trade union groups that it should be published in full. But factory occupations continued, in significant numbers, long after I had ceased to be able to follow their progress in detail. For this reason, this essay is merely an introduction, and much more work needs to be done. I hope that some of the key issues are pinpointed here, but I hope with equal force that the omissions of this work provoke the necessary corrections to it.

Much of the data included below comes from participants in a succession of seminars organised by the Institute for Workers' Control, and much of it is not available elsewhere. I have tried to allow these workers to speak in their own voices, and my debt to them is completely obvious.

I wish to thank all of them, and all my colleagues of the Institute, for their example as well as their participation in the continuing discussion of which this volume is only a part.

Chapter 1

Factory Occupations

Before 1971 the vocabulary of sit-ins was hardly ever used in Britain. After that July, it became part of every industrial correspondent's jargon. Factory occupations, "work-ins", experiments in producer co-operation; all were to come to seem almost commonplace once the workers of Upper Clyde Shipbuilders had successfully taken over the gates of their Clydebank yard. UCS was "occupied" in order to admit television cameras and the press to a shop stewards' press conference. It remained in production, under workers' direct control, as part of a protracted battle to save jobs. But however carefully its workers repeated their insistence on the limited purposes of their initiative, it could not fail to arouse wider hopes, and to conjure up prospects of a very different kind of industrial order.

For more than a month previously the Government had been poised on the brink of this confrontation: the great Scottish shipbuilding consortium had been compelled to go into liquidation, following the rejection of its application for a £6m Government loan. Almost immediately, Secretary of State for Trade and Industry, Mr John Davies, had announced in a parliamentary debate that there would be a special enquiry by four of his nominees, under the chairmanship of Lord Robens. Their report was available in mid-July, but its publication was, it has been reported, delayed for fifteen days "because all available army units were in Northern Ireland".[1] If this rather apocalyptic expectation was nourished in the Cabinet, it was also shared by others.

The Trotskyist newspaper *The Red Mole* greeted the workers' takeover of UCS with the front-page slogan:

> "The Occupation of Clydeside: First Step towards the Scottish Workers' Republic."[2]

Numerous other groups of student socialists, and a whole phalanx of action-oriented TV journalists, held much the same perspective, with varying degrees of enthusiasm.

A decade later, and some few hundred sit-ins to the good, those heady revolutionary hopes or fears have subsided. Yet the factory occupations have not ceased. Work-ins and sit-ins have continually erupted, and narrowly failed to erupt, in almost every corner of the British Isles. From Allis Chalmers, a sleepy-sounding agricultural machine manufactory at Mold, in Flintshire, to the Westland Helicopter plants in Yeovil and Hayes, across to the Fisher-Bendix plant in Liverpool, some firms have been visited and revisited by factory occupations, while many tens of thousands of workers have at one time or another been engaged in them. Even in the middle of a deep slump, in 1980 and 81, sit-ins were still able to win substantial concessions. At Gardners in Manchester, or on the P & O Line Irish ferries from Liverpool, sit-ins could show a capacity to attract enthusiastic support from people in many different unions and workplaces.

This remarkable upsurge has also involved an extraordinarily extended movement of support from workers not directly involved in the disputes at issue, and indeed it is fair to guess that in all probability the numbers of those who have contributed financially to the support of their embattled colleagues must be counted in millions, while those who have taken part in various types of active demonstration of sympathy and solidarity must certainly number, at a conservative estimate, hundreds of thousands.

Thus, the words "sit-in" and "work-in" have not entered the language as idle coinages: they have fought their way into people's imaginations, and the result is that working men and women now see all sorts of possibilities of action and redress in a variety of predicaments which have hitherto, in the recent past, for them spelt only submission. And yet the direct revolutionary confrontation which the Cabinet feared and manoeuvred for a full fortnight to avoid, and which the young left aspired to join, or sometimes, with undergraduate arrogance, to lead, has not come about.

Does this mean that the device of factory occupation, remembered in the popular histories only at times of great social upheaval and collapse, such as the near-revolutionary stresses of Gramsci's Turin,[3] or of France during the upsurge of the Popular Front (or again in 1968);[4] or recorded by scholars as part of a particular culture of trade union radicalism such as marked the development of motor unionism in the USA;[5] was, in placid England and its principalities, accepted by the authorities and domesticated in the process?

If sit-ins have become common since 1971, they were not totally unknown before then.[6] Indeed, there have been somewhat similar initiatives ever since the dawn of the industrial revolution, when "masters" confronted "workmen" who had but the brittlest respect for the "discipline" of the modern factory system, and a healthy folk-memory, if not direct personal experience, of freer ways and styles of life. During the Luddite insurrections in Nottinghamshire, Yorkshire and Derbyshire, the two cultures of work came into dramatic collision, and therefore the fact is misremembered in school books. But in spite of the appearances, no permanent peace resulted from the pacification of that conflict, and it has burst out again and again across the years. The plain truth is that working people have always resented having masters. They have continued this resentment through the years when masters learned to call themselves "employers" and it continues even now their "managers" have learned to operate through functionaries who have read degree courses in human relations.

There is a quarry of experience of this conflict in the history of the Owenite movement, culminating in the struggles of the Grand National Consolidated Trades Union. In Derby, membership of this association was seen as a challenge to managerial prerogatives, and a great lock-out was instigated, at the expense of 15,000 men and women. Their spokesmen appealed to the "men of Nottingham, Leicester, Macclesfield, Manchester, Congleton and Leek", not for charitable maintenance, but for "such machines as may be of instant use" to establish the co-operative commonwealth in Derby.

The optimism of Owen and his co-thinkers was not to be justified by immediate events, which brought repression and the deportation of the Tolpuddle Martyrs. Yet in the long-term Owen's ideas were not to be dismissed.

Directly in the short term they were transmuted, rather than abandoned. The 1844 Rochdale experimenters in consumer co-operation set up their shop, not in order to enter the retail trade and prosper, but with the deliberate intention of collecting together sufficient funds to be able to begin direct production on their own account. Producer co-operation encounters many hazards, and the co-operative commonwealth did not come into being in Rochdale either. But nor was its pursuit abandoned.

In his study of the growth of British producer co-operatives in the latter half of the nineteenth century, Fred Boggis records numerous cases in which strike action resulted in the formation of co-operatives.[7] In 1866, the Glasgow Co-operative Coopers were formed after such a dispute: while in 1872, the Scottish Co-operative Ironworks Society grew out of the Engineers' short-time movement.

> "In 1873 when the workers in the lock trade in Walsall were on strike, their demand was for a 10 per cent increase and the introduction of a uniform trade price list. Agreement was apparently reached but after the return to work the employers refused to implement the list prices. The dispute dragged on with some

workers returning to the firm in dispute until about twenty strikers were left out. What happened to the hard core of the strikers is recounted in this way:

"These (workers) were spotted and refused employment; so the trades council, after paying strike pay for about 17 weeks, decided to recommend the union to support the out-of-work men in forming a Co-operative Padlock Society. The initiative was left to the men, but they were helped largely by a gentleman in the town who used his influence on their behalf. Several unions including the locksmiths', took up shares or gave donations; and certain individuals in the town helped in the same way."

In 1890, as part of the upsurge which was triggered by the growth of new unionism, the London Leather Manufacturers' Co-op, the Co-operative Cabinet Makers of Bradford, the Manchester Billiard Table Makers and the Stick and Cane makers of East London all went into production in their own account as a result of stalemate in, or employer discrimination after, strikes.

Other East End sweated trades were too dispersed or ill-organised to permit strikes, but nonetheless set out to form co-operatives in order to put an end to the gross exploitation which they suffered at the hands of small-scale private employers. So, in 1889, were formed the Co-operative Bass Dressers, the Productive Co-operative Cabinet-makers' Society and (the following year) the Co-operative Bedroom Suite Manufacturing Society. Outside London, co-ops of nailmakers had arisen in Dudley and Bromsgrove, of mat-manufacturers at Long Melford, and of factory-based shoe-makers in Northamptonshire.

The propaganda for such co-operation was nothing if not direct: it may be summed up very fairly in the notions of E.O. Greening:

"a. Workers might regain possession of the implements of production which they lost in the Industrial Revolution;
b. The basic conception of democracy, namely, government by the consent of the governed, should be established in industry;
c. The greatest common measure of liberty and freedom in industry might be secured by this industrial self-determination;
d. The status of the worker might be raised from wage-earner to

Conscious Co-partner;
e. Pride of craft, largely destroyed by machine production, might be restored in a workshop which engendered collective pride in product and organisation;
f. Workers might participate in the surplus arising from their associated endeavour;
g. Consciousness of personal responsibility might be developed through worker direction and finance of the undertaking."

Writing in 1910 during the ferment which seized the South Wales Miners in the earliest moments of the syndicalist movement and the "great unrest" Tom Mann took up the call made by Christian Socialists two decades earlier by launching the appeal "Why not a cooperative mine?"

Although each of these initiatives arose in particular circumstances, one thing is common to all the people involved in them. In private capitalist enterprise, the goals of limited liability companies did not at the turn of the century, and do not today include any deliberate commitments to the personal growth and development of their employees. Still less do they admit that such employees have any right to share in determining policy, controlling its implementation, or electing or dismissing its directors. Men and women are not, however, 'hands'; still less 'cogs'; but people, capable of choice and intelligent discrimination: each harbouring a vast potential for self-discovery in social involvement, if only the opportunity were offered. Overwhelmingly, the opportunity has been withheld.

Sometimes workers have pursued one means of redress for this disability, sometimes another, but always the fundamental indignity has remained. While work has been socialised into greater, more diverse and yet more integral collectives, the control of industrial enterprise has never ceased to be fundamentally a private area. Competition has concentrated this area, but private it has remained. As mergers and drastic competitive pressures have, to a greater or lesser degree, brought about the demise, over a century, of the individual entrepreneur in one trade after another, so we have seen the emergence of a succession of forms of corporate business life. These have given rise to widely different styles of managerial government: but all of them have been, in the last analysis, authoritarian in their diverse forms. They have depended upon a power which has never been anything but external to the working collective. Capital has always been materialised from outside the workforce to "employ" it, always insisting, as Ralph Waldo Emerson had it, that "Things are in the saddle, and ride mankind".

If the workers of the cotton trade of the time of Arkwright and Adam Smith resented the little masters who could lord it over a watermill and a couple of hundred "servants" and apprentices, the kinds of dominance which have become technically feasible in an age of computers and atomic power remain no more fundamentally acceptable to those over whom they rule. It is awareness of this basic inequality which has given rise to the discussion of a whole succession of proposals for "industrial democracy". Some of these have been advanced in order to find ways of democratising industry, and some have been canvassed by others in order the better to prevent it from being democratised. This debate has been an important part of the climate in which work-ins and sit-ins have become thinkable to modern workpeople.

But the modern movement for workers' control has begun its emergence in remarkable conditions: nearly three decades of relatively full-employment based on the transformation of the economy in radical new technologies, and the containment of the world's political structure in the uneasy framework of the Cold War. During the first half of the century, world wars recurrently took their cull of many of the most generous and clever young men of every contending nation. After thermonuclear explosions in the USA and the USSR, such relatively controlled bloodletting became impossible, since future contests must involve universal destruction. Peace and economic development thus became settled expectations in the advanced countries. During that time there has been a revolution in basic educational provision. We have seen the growth of a large stratum of highly qualified technical workers, many of whom are deployed in industries which are capital-intensive to an unprecedented degree. This has been followed by the extension of trade union organisation and modes of thought into areas far beyond the traditional limits of working-class institutions. What is not quite so clear is how far these processes have modified the machinery of Government and the possibilities of industrial reform within the given political process. Because this structure remains opaque to ordinary working people, it has been given the benefit of recurrent doubts. But if working people have been reluctant to accept the revolutionary assumptions of the young left, all the evidence points to the growth of their dissatisfactions, which are partially reflected in the actions discussed below.

Many things have changed since the 1830s. All the more remarkable, one might think, is the degree of continuity between our days and those.

This little book seeks to explore some of the strengths and limitations of the modern sit-in movement, in the context of its contribution to the over-arching argument about industrial democracy.

Footnotes
1. Jack McGill: *Crisis on the Clyde,* Davis-Poynter, 1973, p.101.
2. *The Red Mole,* Vol.2, No.13, 15th July, 1971, p.1.
3. Cf. Paolo Spriano: *The Occupation of the Factories — Italy 1920,* Pluto Press, 1975. Also Antonio Gramsci: *Soviets in Italy,* Institute for Workers' Control, Pamphlet No.11.
4. Cf. Andree Hoyles: *Imagination in Power,* Spokesman, 1973.
5. Cf. Walter Linder: *The Great Flint Sit-down Strike Against GM,* Solidarity Pamphlet No.31, 1969. Also Art Preis: *Labour's Giant Step,* Pathfinder Press, 1968.
6. Knowles, in his authoritative study, *Strikes,* confines himself to recording the fact of the miners' "stay-down" stoppages in the middle 'thirties. Arthur Horner, in his *Incorrigible Rebel* (MacGibbon and Kee, 1960) says that the Welsh staydown strikes were modelled on a Hungarian initiative (pp.133-8). Montague Slater's *Stay Down Miner* (Lawrence and Wishart, 1936) still makes compelling reading on this desperate crop of struggles. A

FACTORY OCCUPATIONS

fictional model for the more recent upsurge was provided by two very striking TV "documentary" style plays, by Jim Allen: *The Big Hewer,* which was broadcast by the BBC, and *The Big Flame,* which was also put out by the BBC during February 1969. This last play dealt with an imaginary workers' takeover of the Liverpool docks.
7. Fred Boggis: *Workers' Co-operatives: A Vital Experiment in Participation in Industry,* edited by Campbell Balfour, Croom Helm, 1973, pp.21-55.

Chapter II

UCS:
A Lame Duck Takes Wing

On June 14th, 1971, the British Government decided to withhold financial assistance which had been requested by the Directors of Upper Clyde Shipbuilders, thus allowing the company to go into liquidation. That evening, Tony Benn spoke to the workers' representatives. He was reported next morning in these terms:

> "Mr Anthony Wedgwood Benn, shadow spokesman on employment and industry, was loudly cheered at a meeting of Clydeside shop stewards in Clydebank last night when he endorsed the proposed trade union action of 'sitting in' in the Upper Clyde Shipbuilding yard threatened with closure.
>
> 'This is a decision you have taken and it is for you to decide', said Mr Benn. 'Your decision not to evacuate the yard is absolutely justified in the circumstances.'
>
> Just as in the case of Rolls Royce, the Government had made an appalling blunder over UCS and would have to reverse their course. He had been expecting the news for 12 months, but he did not think the reason given by Mr Davies for the liquidation of UCS stood up to one moment's examination."[1]

The original suggestion that the workpeople counter dismissals by 'staying put' and working on, had been advanced by Sammy Barr, the convenor of one of the yards constituting the consortium. Apparently it provoked widely different reactions. There were some enthusiasts, but also many voluble sceptics. Yet obviously threatened closures could not sensibly be met by withdrawal of labour, since withdrawal of labour was the precise aim intended by the opposition. Ruling out strike action, more and more workers came to the view that the choice lay between a straightforward sit-in and

Sammy Barr's proposals, unless defeat were to be acknowledged from the beginning. A sit-in would need to be maintained for a very long time, judged its opponents. The Labour-force, recruited from a wide area, scattered around the region, would find it difficult to maintain such an action for weeks, never mind months. But a 'work-in' might, just might, catch people's imaginations and attract that political support, based on a real shift of public opinion, which alone could over-rule a Government decision.

During the week after Tony Benn's visit, mass meetings were held in every one of the yards, and the idea of 'working-in' was carried in each of them. A co-ordinating committee of all the shop stewards in the consortium began to plan to give it reality.

After more than a month of feverish activities by the workers, during which the former Labour Minister of Technology continuously defended their proposals for an occupation of the plant, the Government announced, on July 29th, that two of the four UCS yards were to be closed and sold off.

The next day UCS workers seized control of the gates of the threatened John Brown yard, and defied a ban by the recently appointed liquidator on a shop stewards' press conference called within the workplace. At a mass-meeting of the 3,500 workers in the yard, Jimmy Reid, the chairman of the joint co-ordinating committee for the whole UCS consortium, and an AUEW shop steward, reported on the results of the meeting between the stewards and the Government at which the workpeople had been informed of the proposed closures, which entailed the loss of 6,000 jobs directly, and many thousands more indirectly.

> "This is the first campaign of its kind in trade unionism", he said. "We are not going on strike. We are not even having a sit-in. We do not recognise that there should be any redundancies and we are going to 'work-in'.
>
> "We are taking over the yards because we refuse to accept that faceless men can take these decisions. We are not strikers. We are responsible people and we will conduct ourselves with dignity and

discipline . . . There will be no hooliganism, there will be no vandalism, and there will be no bevvying.

"We are not the wildcats, we want to work. The real wildcats are in Number Ten, Downing Street. they are the hardest-faced bunch of political gangsters I have ever met. They make Al Capone and his gunmen look like a troop of Boy Scouts. The biggest mistake we could make is to lie down, capitulate and grovel to them."[2]

So began the 'work-in' which was to transform the nature of the struggle against unemployment and dismissals in Britain.

There was no affray. Quietly, stewards replaced the gate-man, who simply withdrew on request. Working four-hour rotas, the stewards controlled everything and every person entering or leaving the yards. Consultation with the police revealed that they had no intention of intervening, provided there were no disturbances. The action was to carry on until October 1972, when all four yards involved were saved, and over £47 million of Government money committed to the rescue. During the whole time, the organisation developed by the workers remained in full force, in spite of its involvement in a punishing campaign of public relations which became ever more demanding.

The Crisis in Shipbuilding

Before redundancies were announced in the shipyards, one man in ten in Glasgow's region was already unemployed. Closure of the yards would have created a considerable "knock-on" effect, taking out jobs in a wide range of ancillary industries which were, to a greater or lesser extent, keyed into shipbuilding.

Shipbuilding in Britain had entered a general crisis. For a decade and a half after the Second World War, things had drifted comfortably: but by 1965 Britain produced only 10% of world shipping, as contrasted with 41% in 1949. The story has, alas, become commonplace. Old, under-capitalised plant in Britain was competing against aggressively managed modern equipment abroad, and, increasingly obviously, it was failing.

In 1966 a Government Committee under Lord Geddes reported that British shipyards could not take advantage of the world demand for merchant shipping, because they were both insufficiently specialised and insufficiently concentrated, to develop adequate skills in management, marketing, design, development, purchasing or accounting. Hence the Government of the day intervened, establishing a Shipbuilding Industry Board (SIB) to provide financial aid, and subsequently, through its agency, creating the Upper Clyde Shipbuilders Consortium (UCS) in 1967.[3].

Comprising the new group were: Fairfields, an experiment in joint control involving 50% of Governmental shares and some considerable trade union investment; John Brown's renowned but ramshackle Clydebank yard (with two lesser appendages); Connell's Scotstoun yard; Alexander Stephens' Govan yard, adjoining Fairfields; and Yarrows, an admiralty contractor which soon hived off from UCS after modernising itself under the auspices of the Consortium. As the secretary of the Institute for Workers' Control reported:

> "Despite its ambitious conception, the Upper Clyde Shipbuilders Group was launched on very flimsy foundations. The old owners were only too pleased to get out and to receive compensation for doing it. Some of the yards had practically no orders on hand while the others had order books consisting almost entirely of loss-making contracts; these contracts subsequently lost 12 million pounds. On top of this the yards, apart from Govan (Fairfields), were in a state of dilapidation, full of old and out-of-date equipment often badly laid out. To add to the Shipbuilders' (UCS) initial difficulties many of the executives in the former companies continued in office with UCS, brought their old authoritarian methods into the new concern and found it easier to squabble amongst themselves than to co-operate in developing an integrated structure for the new concern.
>
> The first managing director of UCS, A.E. Hepper, a successful stocking manufacturer, added to the burdens of the concern by filling the order books with further loss-making contracts. As a consequence, not only were there no funds available for much needed equipment, but, through an acute shortage of working capital, the company very soon plunged into a serious financial crisis in early 1969. It was only rescued by a loan from the

UCS: A LAME DUCK TAKES WING

Government of 7 million pounds on top of grants of 5 million pounds from the Board (SIB) and a further 3 million pounds the SIB agreed to subscribe for additional share capital. The Minister of Technology, Anthony Wedgwood Benn, insisted on the introduction of new management and working methods, which involved provision for redundancies. The trade unions accepted these redundancies with great reluctance, but in a situation where general unemployment was not nearly as high as it was soon to become. However, they were able to negotiate higher wage rates as the price for accepting redundancies and new working methods.

A new managing director, Ken Douglas, an experienced and able shipbuilder from Austin Pickergills, was appointed, and he quickly won the support and confidence of the men. He inherited, then, an ill-assorted order book of ships of widely different types and sizes, many of which were still lossmaking. Douglas was instrumental in rationalising largely into cargo ships of standard design which allowed for much more straight-forward operations. Throughput of steel increased in 1970 from 887 tons per week to an average of 1300 tons the week before the liquidation of UCS was announced; 3 ships were completed in 1968, 12 were launched in 1970 and 15 were expected in 1971. Trading losses had fallen from 12 million pounds to 3 million pounds in a year and profits were confidently expected in 1972. After all the pain and sacrifice the yards were, at last, full of confidence for the future of shipbuilding on the Upper Clyde. The dashing of these expectations was a key factor in the workers' sharp and angry reaction to the Government axe after the initial shock and disbelief had passed."

Why, then, did the Government take the decision to cut down UCS just when it was beginning to stand on its own feet? Extracts from a very significant document which throws considerable light on official motivation were published in *The Guardian* in June 1971. The complete text was subsequently released to the public by the shop stewards. It consisted of a letter circulated by Nicholas Ridley to some colleagues in the Conservative Shadow Cabinet in December 1969. Mr Ridley was the Opposition main spokesman on shipbuilding at the time and his report was the result of a brief meeting he had attended with Ken Douglas and a more lengthy conference with Sir Eric Yarrow, who had been hostile to UCS from the outset. Nicholas Ridley recommended that no more Government money be given to UCS, particularly as their wage rates were pushing up the rates of the Scott Lithgow Group on the Lower Clyde, and he insisted that a Government "butcher" should be put in to cut up UCS if the Conservatives were returned to power.

John Davies, the Minister of Trade and Industry, had denied all knowledge of the Ridley Report, but nevertheless its author was appointed to a key position in the Department of Trade and Industry by Edward Heath: and thereafter events followed remarkably closely to the pattern laid down in the Ridley document. Ridley himself played a central part in suspending Government credit guarantees to shipowners and this was the death blow to the prospects of UCS. It meant that shipowners ceased paying instalments for work completed on ships under construction and that, in turn, UCS were unable to pay their own creditors. As a consequence vital supplies were held back and the work flow was interrupted at a time when the concern was on the point of breaking through to viability. UCS were forced to apply for a further Government loan of £6 million in May 1971, but John Davies reaffirmed that no more public money would be given to UCS and that instead a liquidator must be appointed.

> "The Government was somewhat taken aback by the tremendous outcry against the decision and agreed to appoint a four-man enquiry . . . (This) reported, after only six weeks of not very intensive work. Their report consisted simply of four pages. It recommended that the Clydebank and Scotstoun yards be run down as current orders were completed and that only the Govan yard (with Stephens yard as an ancillary) be kept open. Even this small concession was barbed: the reprieved yard would operate with a reduced labour force, subject to more intensive discipline and renegotiated wage rates. No arguments or factual documentation were given to support any of these sweeping conclusions. The Government refused to publish any such information, without giving any plausible reasons, and despite insistent demands that this be done.
>
> It is perfectly clear that the 'Four Wise Men', as they inevitably came to be known, were under no pressure from the Government to offer evidence which might frustrate its own clear intentions. If the workers at UCS were to win any reprieve, they had a fight on

their hands, since before they could secure a hearing for their reasoned case, they needed to buy time to delay an imminent execution."[4]

This was the immediate background to the declaration of the work-in. But things had been stirring in the wider labour movement, as well.

A Helpful Example

The trade union movement learns by experience, and sometimes it learns almost as much from failure as from success. The remarkable successes of the UCS workers were themselves partly attributable to lessons drawn from just such an earlier failure. Contrary to widespread belief, the initiative at UCS was not the first to be taken by the modern movement. The Institute for Workers' Control was formed in 1968, with a view to popularising ideas of industrial democracy. It was first involved in action of this kind in the Summer of 1969, when workers at the GEC plants in Liverpool, threatened by factory closures and rationalisations, appealed for its help in providing specialist services and advice to assist a wholesale occupation of Merseyside GEC plants, which were then to be run by a combined shop stewards' committee. Members of the Institute's Council made many visits to Liverpool, and were able to form clear impressions of the difficulties involved in this strategy.[5]

In mid-August, the GEC stewards had announced their plans for a workers' takeover, which, they said, would begin on September 19th. Occupation passes were printed in readiness for the day. There followed a storm of press publicity, which had the merit of popularising (albeit inadvertently) the idea of workers' occupations, among people far removed from Liverpool and its particular problems. At meetings of the stewards, however, it soon became clear, that "working-in" at GEC was fraught with very great difficulties, and that the management were persistently, and not unskilfully, exploiting these difficulties. Among the questions which workers pressed upon their representatives were a number of recurrent problems.

What, they asked, would happen to the entitlement to redundancy pay of those who took part in the occupation? What were the stewards' plans for ensuring continued supplies of raw materials and power? How would they be paid, and how would they purchase supplies? What would be done with the existing management, and how would charges of trespass be dealt with? But of all the questions, the most insistent was, what protection would workers have if they were injured during work organised by a workers' occupation, and by what means could they be insured?

The GEC stewards tried to secure answers to some of these technical problems from sympathetic trade union officers, but they were never able to present convincing blue-prints for the solution of the majority of the questions. The most difficult questions were perhaps the easiest to answer: the workers would have been paid, if at all, out of solidarity funds, and they would almost certainly have been generously forthcoming. They would have been provisioned, if at all, as a result of solidarity action in other relevant plants and distribution services, which would have required the extension of active solidarity by trade unionists in other sectors of the economy. This would not have proved easy. Charges of trespass could only be brought if the use of force to remove the workers was contemplated by authority, so that litigation was not likely to be an immediate contingency, since such a battle, however it went, could only result in a great moral defeat for the authorities themselves. To the problem of insurance, there was no solid answer, at the time, even though several people thought they had found one.

In retrospect, the opinion of both the IWC and a number of GEC workers themselves was that in an industry such as that involved in Liverpool in which there were large-scale difficulties in securing both inputs of material and outlets to the market, "working-in" was an unrealistic goal, and that the same result could have been achieved by a sit-in which announced its intention of working on once the problems of supplies and services had been solved, with the help of the trade unions. Such action would have called for an enormous effort by the Labour Movement, but it could well have succeeded.

But the GEC workforce was divided. The most intensively organised plant was at Netherton, and, apart from its aircraft section, this was scheduled for complete closure. Napiers, also well represented, was also marked down to be finished. But the least organised sector, the English Electric factory in the East Lancs Road, was only to share 300 dismissals among 8,000 employed there, Not unexpectedly, when the steward's decision came to be reversed, it was some of the workers in this section who began the rebellion. They were stimulated by intensive hostile coverage in the newspapers, coupled with a "personal" letter from the management which was also reproduced in the *Liverpool Echo*. Armed with a megaphone, they advanced on a platform at the mass meeting of September 17th, and successfully moved a resolution annulling the work-in. Only two days remained before the occupation was due, and these were filled with celebrations in the newspapers, concerning the fundamental good sense and amenability of British workers, who were, it seems, not quite so bad after all.

Yet even the collapse of the Liverpool work-in was anything but a defeat, for it sowed ideas which were soon to grow and bear fruit. One of those who was profoundly influenced by the Liverpool events was Tony Benn. At the time he was Minister of Technology, and thus responsible for industry. He visited the plants on the day that the proposed occupation was to have taken place, and was intercepted and conducted around by the shop stewards' committee. He has subsequently commented upon the deep impression that this visit made on him, and it certainly influenced his attitudes to the predicament faced by the men of Clydeside two years later.

Why did the work-in work?

How, then, did the shop stewards at UCS succeed in establishing an occupation by the workpeople when Liverpool had previously failed? In 1969, national unemployment queues totalled more than 600,000 people, with some 30,000 of these on Merseyside. by 1971 more than 800,000 were out of work in Britain, almost 130,000 of whom were in Scotland. Both areas had a strongly militant tradition, and both had produced able leaders, so that neither of these conditions can explain the discrepancy between the two experiences. There was one major technical difference: at UCS the workers found themselves in control of an asset which became more valuable with each day of work — the ninety million pounds' worth of shipping under construction, which the pilots could always refuse to take down the Clyde until a satisfactory agreement was reached. There was also an important political difference: the Labour Government had fallen, and one of its most prominent and able spokesmen had become convinced that the Labour Party's future depended on its willingness to become the champion of the cause of industrial democracy.

It is perfectly clear, also, that leaders of the UCS initiative were well aware of the problems which had worried the Liverpool stewards before them. (They should have been: 2,000 copies of the IWC pamphlet recording the story of the GEC struggles were distributed in Glasgow between June 14th and July 30th.) Speaking at an IWC Conference in Newcastle-upon-Tyne,[6] Jimmy Airlie summed up the ideas of the Glasgow men in characteristically shrewd terms:

> "It was not a simple matter, saying we would work-in: we realised that there would be certain problems, and one of the problems would be the questions that were raised before, during the planned GEC takeover, such as whether the workers could draw their

redundancy pay, and what should be done about insurance and so on.

We attempted to answer these problems with our successes in the struggle. Of course, the Government solved some of these problems when they set up their Committee of Enquiry, the 'Four Wise Men', who gave their report which in effect meant the butchery of the industry, slashing it from eight and a half thousand workers down to two and a half thousand, and demanding the acceptance of worse conditions, wages structures and so on. This Report really hardened the attitude of the workers. So the joint shop stewards' committee met and formulated the plan of the work-in, resulting in our taking over the gates and in effect saying we would control the yard. When we called a mass meeting of the workers, we got a unanimous decision to that effect. Then the questions which the joint shop stewards had to resolve were very complicated."

First among these complex issues was the problem of what to do about redundancy:

"because many workers were liable to receive redundancy pay, and subsequently the liquidator did declare 800 workers redundant. So we had a debate: and it was that kind of sharp but constructive debate in which some of the lads were arguing, and understandably, that the men who were declared redundant should not accept redundancy pay because this would be de facto acceptance of redundancy. But we argued that it would be quite wrong to look at things that way: that if the State wanted to pay a man around £800 that was its business: all that we were asking was that after he was paid his money he should still keep coming into the factory and we would alleviate his hardship."

The next major topic to be resolved was that of insurance:

"Lads came forward to say, 'What will happen if we get injured at work?' Our answer was: 'Look brother, every day you go to work you're liable to get injured, so we're saying to you, don't get injured. But if you do, we'll give you this guarantee, that no one will suffer as a result of the work-in, or, if there is any suffering it will be on an equal basis, and because you're working-in you'll be working on the same conditions as if you were working out.'"

Critics on the "far" left have frequently claimed that UCS succeeded because it was a pseudo-action, not a "real" one. Such criticisms should certainly be studied, but it must be said at the outset that they do not carry conviction. Once again, Jimmy Airlie provides a convincing reply.

> "One of the main criticisms that we hear from certain quarters of the Labour movement has been to the effect that the work-in has been 'pseudo-revolutionary'. Such critics say that we have been conning the workers, that we have set up something which is really only a big public relations job; and they tell us that we should sit-in, not work-in. In answer to all this, first of all, I would say that anybody who ever worked in a shipyard would not talk about sitting-in, but in any case we felt it would be wrong, tactically, and that ideologically it wasn't the right position.
>
> I must stress that we have always said that we feel that the work-in applies to our particular position: we don't say that it will be the formula of every type of struggle. Sometimes, the sit-in is the best thing that can be done. The work-in suits some lads because of the nature of their particular industry. In other places it would not be a work-in or a sit-in: in the big multi-combines I would argue that with all the difficulties they've got with the combines, if there is a combine committee that operates effectively with a rank and file shop stewards committee, if you take over one factory you can at the same time appeal to all the other factories who'd all be stopping: that's the approach I would argue if I was working in a multi-combine factory. There's no one way to battle with redundancy. The only constant fact is that you struggle, because only through struggle can you develop the understanding of the workers"

Whether or not the workers of West Central Scotland shared Jimmy Airlie's precise notions of the implications of these actions, the popular appeal, which they made, on their own merits, was electric. The contrast, in the minds of these workers, was not how far the work-in fell short of some imaginary revolution, but how far it surpassed the previous overwhelmingly passive practice during arguments on redundancy. This, Airlie pointed out;

> "Previously, in the West Central belt of Scotland, up and down this country, we have had bitter experiences of mass redundancies and closures, all of which have always been met with the time-worn formula that the MPs and the local full-time union officials would be called in to meet with the Employers' Association, who would then meet the representatives of the Department of Trade and Industry: but all the time the workers would be outside the gates waiting on their fates. The UCS work-in has been revolu-

UCS: A LAME DUCK TAKES WING

tionary in the sense that it has shown, here was a workforce which stood up to say 'We have hopes, we have aspirations, and no one is going to negotiate above our heads: we're taking control of the yards and to move us you'll have to come in and get us!' I would suggest that whatever criticism may be made that event was revolutionary."

Around UCS there was a threefold mobilisation of dramatic proportions.[7]

First, the Scottish trade unions rallied in two vast demonstrations which had enormous political meaning, and the Scottish TUC was drawn into a major campaign of action on behalf of UCS. Later, at the prompting of Tony Benn, this body successful carried through the first social audit to be commissioned by British unions, which itself helped to create a rallying focus for the fight against unemployment. We shall discuss this further in Chapter VI.

Second, the Labour Movement from all over Britain was inspired to contribute enormous sums of money to maintain the work-in, and the initiative spread to other plants in different industries, including concerns which supplied the yards.

Third, the political institutions of Labour were drawn into the struggle, formally endorsing the UCS initiative and at the same time demanding a nationalised shipbuilding industry. Indeed, the Parliamentary Labour Party took up this cause even before the Party Conference, which is an unusual initiative for such a cautious body to make. None of this is in any way negligible.

These overall gains were undoubtedly affected by the very particular problems raised by the crisis on the Clyde, which, as a one-time strong point of the Scottish economy, became, in its decline, a symbol for all the more general difficulties of the Scots, arousing a very general national concern, which was reflected throughout the Scottish press, including some of the most conservative newspapers.* Yet at the same time

---
*Not all, however. Some were disgracefully unfair.

that UCS seemed to Scotland a dreadful warning of the likely prospects of other Scottish industries, it was also a most unpleasant omen for the rest of the shipbuilding industry throughout Britain. Extremely dependent on state contracts and direct aid, this declining sector was made more aware of its vulnerability by the apparent brutality of the Government's decision to close the Upper Clyde. Such pressures ensured from the beginning that the UCS men would receive wide publicity, and this was brilliantly exploited by their rank-and-file leaders, notably by Jimmy Reid.

Yet, although such political gains have deep significance, the trade union scope of the work-in inevitably remained tied to the objective of rescuing as many jobs as possible within the available structure. The declared aim of the work-in at its commencement, was to keep open all four shipyards comprising UCS and to maintain in employment the total labour force at the moment of liquidation, 8,500. In accordance with this aim, workers were advised to refuse to accept dismissal notices (although, as Jimmy Airlie pointed out, they were encouraged to accept payment of redundancy monies) and to remain at work under the authority of the shop stewards' co-ordinating committee, which supplemented the dispute benefit they were receiving from their unions by a weekly payment which equalled their previous half-year's average weekly earnings. About £9,000 a week was paid out throughout the work-in. The co-ordinating committee raised the wherewithal for these payments by its appeal for funds to the Labour Movement, which responded warmly. Support came not only from a cross-section of British trade union and radical organisations, but also from many foreign trade unions.

From inside the yards, each worker paid a levy of 50p a week to the fund. From outside, monies were sent by thousands of individuals. John Lennon sent a bunch of red roses and a large contribution: collections were taken at meetings all over Britain, while donations came from as far away as Australia. (A crop of factory and mine occupations broke out in that country soon after the news of UCS was heard by Australian trade unionists.) Some forty stewards were elected to the co-ordinating committee, which sat continuously in daily meetings, and which heard regular reports from the convenors at the four yards, and from departmental stewards who held weekly meetings of the men in their sections. A finance committee was charged with a whole series of technical duties, such as paying the national insurance stamps of work-in "employees", and with maintaining discretion about the exact state of the treasury for as long as was necessary to prevent the Government from estimating the exact achievement of the work-in. £350,000 was paid out inside the yards in a period of some 40 weeks: at the same time, the UCS workers made generous contributions to appeals by other groups of workers as their initiative began to attract imitators. One estimate of the total fund raised puts it as £485,000.[8] Another guesses "at least half a million".[9]

To maintain good communications, at intervals there were mass meetings in the four separate yards, and from time to time there were general meetings of all workers employed within the consortium.

The work of the yards was carefully regulated to ensure that the liquidator only received what he paid for, and this meant that workers who "worked-in" were sometimes employed in maintaining the work-in itself. To avoid insurance problems, care was taken in the deployment of men who were "working-in". The most careful control was exercised over the deployment of capital equipment, and fully or partially finished ships could only be removed from their construction sites with the approval of the co-ordinating committee. At the same time, labour discipline was maintained by the committee, which drew up a series of rules, including the prohibition of drinking and fighting which was announced by Jimmy Reid at the commencement of the action. The difficulty inherent in the work-in was not however, that such rules needed any elaborate enforcement. On the contrary, so great was the enthusiasm that a major problem became the restraint of production to pre-occupation levels. Obviously, the sooner that existing contracts were completed, the more immediate became the threat of further lay-offs. So the pace of work was restricted, in principle, to that which obtained before the June decision to close the yards.

Constant scrutiny by the media ensured that the workers' successes in overcoming the organisational difficulties which confronted them, many of which were the subject of prolonged public speculation, were borne home not only to other trade unionists, but also to the leading Labour politicians and the Government itself. By the time of the Labour Conference in Autumn 1971, the UCS visiting delegation received an ecstatic welcome.

In February 1972 the Government announced a grant of £35 million towards the reconstitution of three of the four yards, with a promise of additional aid to any prospective buyer of the fourth yard, Clydebank. The three yards, under the auspices of Govan Shipbuilders Ltd., became independently operational with a £35 million Government contribution, on July 1st 1972: Marathon Manufacturing, a rigbuilding company, took over the fourth, with a £12 million grant, on October 10th when the work-in was ended. Altogether the Government was to pay out more than £47 million.

In conventional trade union terms this represented an obvious victory. Not only had a large number of jobs previously considered "terminated" in fact been resumed, but all four yards remained working, with considerable State underpinning provided on the instruction of a Government which had previously been pledged to carry through wholesale economies in subventions to "lame ducks". As a defensive action, undertaken in the immediate interests of the Clyde men themselves, there could be no reasonable doubt that this represented a considerable success. This success was, however, accompanied by a number of concessions exacted during the negotiations, which, unless they could be subsequently reversed, would surely undermine some of the traditional trade union controls within the yards. These concessions included, at Clydebank, a 'no-strike' agreement, an accord about 'flexibility' in manning and demarcation questions and new shift-work arrangements. Naturally, the balance sheet of the effect of such measures may only be elaborated in the total context of the future working of the yards. Without the work-in, though, the redundancy programme would have been a far more decisive attack on basic trade union rights, and this was quite obvious to the workpeople, even when they were worried about the erosion of long-established work-procedures. But how could it be evaluated in political terms, in the context of the overall struggle against unemployment and its social causes?

Footnotes

1. *The Scotsman,* 15th June 1971.
2. Alasdair Buchan: *The Right to Work — The Story of the Upper Clyde Confrontation,* Calder and Boyars, 1972, p.14.
3. Cf. Jack McGill: *Crisis on the Clyde,* Davis-Poynter, 1973.
4. Ken Fleet: an unpublished brief for the UCS social audit, organised by the STUC.
5. Cf. *GEC-EE Workers' Takeover,* IWC Pamphlet No.17, 1969.
6. Held at Henderson Hall, Newcastle University, on January 8th-9th 1972.
7. For an account of these responses, see Jack McGill: *Crisis on the Clyde,* Davis-Poynter, 1973, Chapters II et seq. Also W. Thompson and Finlay Hart: *The UCS Work-In,* Lawrence and Wishart, 1972.
8. Terry Bishop: When the Workers Take Control, *Personnel Management,* journal of the IPM: March 1973.
9. North East TU Studies Unit: *Workers' Occupations and the North-East Experience,* 1976, p.20.

Chapter III

Some Lessons

There were some socialists for whom the Communist affiliations of the two best-known spokesmen of the yards, the fluent Jimmy Reid, who became both a highly effective TV personality, and a university rector, as a result of his part in the struggle, and the more reticent Jim Airlie, a solid organiser of considerable resource and skill, were sufficient evidence of their perfidy to guarantee the failure of any enterprise in which they might become engaged. Groupings like the Socialist Labour League (later to style itself the Workers' Revolutionary Party) maintained a daily barrage of hostile commentary[1] on the alleged "sell-outs" and "carve-ups" which were speculatively attributed to the work-in's leaders. Undoubtedly, with critics like these, the UCS stewards could be forgiven if they became impatient of advice from outside their own ranks.

Yet there were other voices on the left which offered counsel which was better-meant, and more rational.

It is perfectly true that shipbuilding is an unusual industry, in which construction is a long-term affair. Because capital was heavily committed at the moment of liquidation, the liquidator was compelled to strive to salvage what he could for the UCS creditors, so he was interested in securing the speediest possible completion of the vessels under construction. Obviously, if the workers could "employ" their redundant colleagues to speed up the process, he was unlikely to have grounds for complaint. There was, therefore, a temporary overlap of interest between workpeople, liquidator and top management on this score. This was what prompted those socialist critics of the UCS struggle, whom we cited above, to urge an end to ship construction, and the inauguration of a straightforward "sit-in".[2]

Yet this was a dogmatic and unhelpful view. The appeal of the idea of a "work-in" was its power to explain to millions of ordinary workers that workers' control of dismissals is entirely possible, that workers can veto manpower policies of which they disapprove, and that the power of management is only unchallenged where trade unionists have decided not to challenge it.

In this connection it was, however, unfortunate that some UCS workers felt it necessary to deny that they were exercising "control" over dismissals. The denial stems from respectable motives: such workers use the words "workers' control" to describe what advocates of workers' control call "socialist self-management", or in other words, the democratic adminstration of socialised industry.[3] This is a terminological problem, but it has a political meaning. The Communist Party, in particular, tends, as an organisation, to relegate the idea of workers' control to the socialist future, ruling out serious encroachment of powers within capitalist society: although many individual British Communists, from Tom Mann through to the present day, have always shared the perspectives which unite the modern workers' control movement.

Advocates of workers' control in the contemporary sense preach their doctrine as the aggressive erosion of "managerial" perogatives and powers by trade unions.

Within this view, trade unions should seek to increase the areas of unilateral determination, by workers, of the conditions of their work. Thus, Jack Jones of the Transport and General Workers' Union called for direct workers' control of matters pertaining to health and the enforcement of safety regulations: dockers have for some time effectively controlled all hiring and firing within their industry: decisions about working methods have, in a number of craft trades, long been subject to a more or less effective workers' veto.

This is what the engineers' union were demanding when they insisted that any procedural agreement in the engineering industry should contain "status quo" provisions, so that managers could enforce no changes in working arrangements without first obtaining the workers' consent. Of course, nobody thinks that unions can simply continuously, and step-by-step, encroach all the power in industry until they can run the whole show. Sooner or later, and sooner rather than later, workers' control in the trade union sense comes up against the juridical barrier of the private ownership of industry, and that barrier will only be surmounted by political action, by a change in the law, socialising industrial property. Of course, the strategic aim of workers' control is the self-management of such socialised industry, and this should always be borne in mind.

While important experiments in co-operative production are possible under certain conditions in predominantly capitalist economies, self-management as a general programme is normally linked with various forms of public ownership in which economic enterprises may be organised with greater or lesser degrees of autonomy inside the framework of a variety of types of more or less democratic overall plan. Manifestly, the spokesman of the UCS were right to insist that they could not by an act of collective will levitate the Glasgow-based ship-building industry clear over the manifold problems imposed by a hostile political economy: but it is clear that their very success in establishing a platform for the advocacy of alternative social priorities could have enabled them to speak directly to the need for the alternative institutions which *could* embody such priorities.

Once the upsurge on the Clyde had convinced both the TUC and the Labour Party that shipbuilding should be nationalised, it became possible for the workers in the ship-yards to make recommendations about the type of structure they desired under the new order. Any reluctance to spell out their own demands for democratic control over their industry, once it came into public ownership, would surely bring them unnecessary difficulties later on. This point was very strongly made by Brian Nicholson, a London docker and member of the National Executive of the T&GWU, in a direct appeal to the UCS stewards:

"In taking control of the UCS shipyards the ship-building workers are putting into practice a form of industrial democracy. If this is to be more than a temporary experience, a demonstration which is eventually overtaken by some modified form of orthodox management, it sems to be that the ship-building workers will very soon be asking the question: how should a democratically-run shipyard be organised? And: how can we establish the organisation we desire, in practice?

The dockers' experience suggests very strongly that, if the workers themselves, and their organisations (unions and political parties) have engaged in a thorough discussion at all levels, then the kind of programme, the kind of demands that emerge, will be the property of the workers themselves, and that as such, they will be prepared to fight for them. If you want ship-building — or simply the UCS — to be nationalised, or municipalised, then it is no use (so we learned anyway) leaving it to Whitehall, or even to the national levels ofyour own Party, to draft the details of the management body or bodies which will have authority in your industry. You need your own blueprint, which specifies who has authority, where it comes from, and to whom it is accountable.

That is what we did on the docks. We prepared a document, *The Dockers Next Step*[4] which contained our blueprint. It is not perfect. It may well not be the model of democratic management which you are thinking about. The point is that it is ours; we worked on it, produced it, campaigned for it. The Labour Party and the TGWU both produced programmes which have much in common with our programme, and this fact indicates the way in which a genuine 'public opinion' was forming on this matter in our section of the labour movement.

With the experience now being acquired by the stewards and workers in the present historic act on the Clyde, there is no doubt in my mind that you will reach beyond what we were able to set down in our programme, and that your demands for democratic management will be more precise and directly related to experience than ours could be. But this is my point; set in motion now your discussion of what form of democratic authority you want. Define it and popularise it. We are all engaged in a common fight to replace arbitrary, socially-blind authority, by a responsible, democratically-accountable system of social management. The Clyde workers and the Clyde community have taken a giant stride towards this goal. We are sure to learn great lessons from your experience.

Your struggle for full employment and social costing of economic decisions, expresses the needs and interests of the whole working population. I want to argue that because of the way in which technological change is taking place, the decisions about who builds ships, where they are built, what kind of ships they are, and who owns and operates them, have repercussions throughout the world of labour. We should recognise this fact, and seek to unite and harmonise our separate concerns in order to impose social costing on the whole transport revolution. In this way the solidarity which has been built on the Clyde over the threatened closure of the shipyard, can find expression in very wide sections of the labour movement indeed.

In the past decade or more, a revolution in cargo-handling methods has been introduced, mainly through the competitive struggle of shipowners for traffic. We have had the growth of containerisation, bulk-carriers, lighter-abroad-ship, and air-freight. If shipbuilding is to remain and prosper on the Clyde (and I support without reservation your demands in this respect) then some of the work which you do, contributes further to the labour-saving threat which faces maritime and port workers of all kinds. At the same time, it constantly undermines your own position as ship-builders, since one container ship is able to do the work previously done by several conventional ships, and the demand for new ships is therefore reduced. The shipyard workers are not of course responsible for the social consequences which affect either themselves or their brothers and sisters in other parts of the transport industry. The decisions are taken by the shipowners, and the dockers can grasp immediately the central point which is being made by the Clydeside workers; that these decisions are taken regardless of social consequences. Dockers and merchant seamen are thrown on the scrapheap as a result of the same process from which the shipyard workers suffer. Shipping companies employ you indirectly, just as they employ dockers and seamen directly.

Moreover, the technical developments in shipbuilding and cargo-handling are changing the geography of the port and industrial landscape. New ports, to handle modern vessels and methods, are being built. There is, of course, no overall socially conscious plan to direct these changes in location. Often they are developed in areas outside those with strong trade union and labour traditions, therefore increasing the arbitrary authority of owners and management.

From this kind of observation, the dockers are moving towards the demand for National Transport Policy. The Clyde workers' demand for social planning can broaden out our whole approach to this. We ought to be demanding that the ordering of ships, the organisation and location of ports, inland freight facilities, steel production, and process industries like oil and chemicals, should all be subject to social control. At the centre of much of this, stands the shipping industry itself. If a publicly-owned and socially accountable shipping industry were created, it could help to give you a steady, phased and relevant stream of orders, and could be held accountable for the social consequences of its developments, as they affected both shipyard workers and all others in transport.

The need for unity amongst working people requires that, recognising our mutual inter-dependence, we now address ourselves concretely to the problem of common policy in the whole field of transport. In this way, we make your struggle directly relevant to the struggle of dockers and other transport workers, and greatly strengthen the bonds of solidarity between us.

I could never have imagined, just one year ago, that I would have an opportunity to address an appeal of this kind to a shipbuilding community. Your problems seemed remote from our problems. Now, in the moment of your adversity, we can recognise the strength and the relevance of your case."[5]

This Appeal remained largely unheard. Unfortunately, no serious attempt was made to consolidate, programmatically, the advances which had been made in the practical struggle. By contrast, shipyard workers at Barrow met with their Member of Parliament, Albert Booth, to work out a detailed blueprint for democracy in a publicly owned industry. Of course, it may be argued that such elaboration was both difficult, and possibly, inexpedient, for the men of UCS during their negotiations with private buyers who might help rescue the yards. This would be a short-sighted view, because the real inducement to encourage potential buyers came not from the uncertain prospect of trade union moderation, but from the highly realistic hope for substantial Governmental assistance. The amounts of such assistance would not contract in the heat of political dispute about the socialist reorganisation of the industry. More likely, untoward agitation of this kind was likely to push the Government into paying more, and paying it more speedily. But even supposing that the negotiations with Mr 'Cashdown' Kelly might have been adversely affected if, at the same time as they were going on, the Labour Party had been considering detailed proposals from the shop stewards for the establishment of industrial democracy in the nationalised shipbuilding industry; it is quite clear that after the settlement this impediment to political advance no longer existed. It was then absolutely possible for the UCS stewards to table their own proposals for the consideration of the whole Labour Movement.

This point was underlined by Robin Murray, in a submission given in evidence to the Scottish TUC's enquiry into the costs of closure of UCS, which concluded with a striking description of self-management in the Yugoslav shipyard at Split.

> "The experience of UCS has provided a case study of the working of private capital. It has been marked by a tradition of incompetent owner family management. The disruptions and costs which have been visited on this capital as a result of its inefficiencies (in market terms) have been born principally by the workers at UCS and the wider public via the state. Redundancy, the devaluation of skills, lower wages, transfers of capital from public to private hands, insecurities: this is one way to run a shipyard and a system.
>
> But there are other ways. The shipyard at Split in Yugoslavia is one example. This yard is 27th in the ranking of world yards. Its annual capacity is 200,000 d.w.t., it employs 4,500 men, it can make prefabricated sections up to 120 tons, and is planning a dry dock capable of taking ships of up to 100,000 d.w.t. It is therefore comparable to UCS.
>
> In this yard workers meet as a collective and elect 76 representatives to the Workers' Council. the percentage poll was 87% in 1966 and 91.2% in 1967. Each representative is elected as representative of a department for a period of two years, the number of representatives for any one department varying with the size of the department. The Workers' Council has six committees (Socio-economic, Personnel, Protection and Safety, Social Standards, Applications and Complaints, and Division of incomes) whose membership is not confined to Council members.
>
> The Workers' Council elects the Managing Board of ten members (plus the General Director ex offico), for one year. No worker is allowed to be on the board for more than two successive

years. The Managing Board has six committees, (Applications and Petitions, Executive Staff Interviewing, Damage and Replacements, Inventories, Skill Assessment, Inventions and Technical Advances.) Meetings of the managing board are usually held every ten to fourteen days.

The General Director is appointed by the Managing Board for four years, as are the fifteen Heads of Department. His job is to run the yard in accordance with the decisions of the Workers' Councils, control the men and machinery, improve production, working methods, and the safety of the workers and to reduce costs. He is required to give all necessary information to the organs of management, report on progress to the managing board, respond to questions, and so on. He meets the Assistant General Director and the Directors of Finance Production, Design, Purchasing and Sales in the *Collegium* which is intended to be a forum of experts.

Each of the 15 departments in the yard has its own Department Workers' Council, elected at the same time and on the same basis as the Central Workers' Council. Each such council has seven committees (Wages, Recruitment and Termination of Employment, Housing, Safety, Applications and Petitions, Damage and Replacements and Discipline).

There is finally a Supervisory Committee which is responsible for seeing that the yard is managed in accordance with its constitution ('Statut') and with the national law.

The shipyard at Split is not a democratic paradigm. As might be expected manual workers tend to vote for white collar workers for the management organs. In 1967 the Managing Board consisted of two engineers (one of whom was the chairman), two technicians, one economist, a female lawyer, three highly skilled workers and one skilled worker. The Central Workers' Council also has (in 1965) a disproportionate number of white collar workers on it (39% of the representatives although they constituted only 13% of the work force). On the Departmental Workers' Councils the disproportions were not so pronounced. Not only, therefore, were manual workers electing white collar workers, but the Managing Director and the Collegium did in practice have a considerable freedom as well as an influence as a pressure group within the yard. The yard is dominated by specialists and professional managers, and of course is subject to the over-arching discipline of the market, (over 10 years up to 1967, 72% of the ships built in the yard were for overseas owners).

Split shows that a large shipyard can be run with formal and indeed some substantial workers' control over the organisation of production and circulation. Such control is in the Yugoslavian context, a real achievement but limited. The rationality of the plan cannot be substituted for the rationality of the market by changing the formal control of production and circulation in one plant. The characteristic deforming features of the market system always tend to impose themselves: over-capacity, crisis, unemployment, spatial and social inequalities, the dessicated work process. The struggle is always to meet these deformations face-to-face; to resist their rationality with another.

Split comes out of the Yugoslavian experience of this struggle. It is specific; its strengths and weaknesses are rooted in that national history. I have cited it as an example of an alternative, not *the* alternative. There would be dangers in trying to imitate Split too directly at UCS.

Indeed the work-in at UCS has been the Clyde workers' own dramatic attempt to defend their definition of economic rationality. To the choices offered them by the market, between one set of owners and another, between the abandonment of their traditional craft veto-powers and redundancy, between lower wages and the dole, they have responded with their own way of putting the question. They have shown that the market itself faces as well as imposes limits, that the market system has to answer as well as ask questions. The UCS workers have put their questions moreover on the basis of their own institutions, their own crisis-authority — the shop steward's committee — and it is this which one might foresee gathering powers (over redundancy, work measurement schemes, shift arrangements, safety and speed of work, production plans, financial goals, movement of materials and equipment, appointments of managers) rather than a formalised and integrated organisational model on the lines of Split. Dual rationalities are reflected in dual structures."[6]

The Split experiment showed that there could be a different basis for the administration of the industry once it was nationalised: but even before the socialisation of industry, workers can encroach some real power, and UCS is a dramatic proof of the fact. Several hundred men at UCS remained at work when their employers said they shouldn't be: the "right to hire and fire" was seized by the workpeople, and effectively exercised for more than a year, during which time, otherwise, hundreds of families would have been forced on to the dole.[7]

This was the immediate and apparent lessons of UCS. Yet is was almost as immediately obvious that the responses of the Clyde men could not be imitated everywhere. As they themselves insisted, the course of action chosen by other workers who were threatened with redundancy was determined by at least two considerations. Firstly, what were the workpeople prepared and able to do? This was likely to vary with trade union strength and self-confidence, itself a product of different cultures and different economic alternatives. It would also reflect the second determinant, fixed in the material possibilities of the industry concerned. Long-range construction projects on a vast scale, and tiny labour-intensive workshops at the other extreme, are ideal ground for work-ins. But in many other areas of industry, sit-ins are obviously far more relevant responses.

Footnotes

1. The main coverage in the Workers' Press resulted in a book: Stephen Johns, *Reformism on the Clyde — The Story of UCS,* Socialist Labour League Pocket Library, No.7, 1973.
2. This was the point of view which was repeatedly pressed in the *Socialist Worker,* the journal of the International Socialists.
3. This distinction is argued at length in Ken Coates and Tony Topham, *The New Unionism,* Penguin Books, 1974.
4. IWC Pamphlet No.12, 1969.
5. Brian Nicholson, *UCS: An Open Letter,* IWC Pamphlet No.27, 1971.
6. *UCS: The Anatomy of Bankruptcy,* Spokesman, 1972.
7. Michael Barratt Brown, *UCS: The Social Audit,* IWC Pamphlet No.26, 1971. See below, pp.87-99.

Chapter IV

Sit-ins

From Clydebank to Alexandria

The movement of straightforward factory occupations, or "sit-ins" began very close indeed to the shadow of UCS, at a former torpedo manufactory known as the Argyle Works in Alexandria, Dumbartonshire, which had been taken over by Plessey's, the electro-communications combine, from the Ministry of Defence.

Alexandria is some 40 minutes by train from Glasgow, in the Vale of Leven, a short trek from Loch Lomond. In late 1971 nearly one in eight of all males in the area was unemployed. As the Scottish newspapers carried daily stories of new closures and threats of lay-offs throughout West Central Scotland, the disquiet in Alexandria naturally increased.

The torpedo factory had been in production from the Second World War until January 1970 and during its later years it had been manufacturing Mark 24 torpedoes for the Royal Navy. At the time that its closure was announced, the plant employed 1,200 men. Plesseys, who also manufactured torpedoes at their plant in Ilford, expressed an interest in taking over and converting the Alexandria factory to develop and manufacture numerically controlled machine tools. They gave out an estimate of 2,000 as being the likely labour force they would require. According to a broadsheet subsequently issued by the workers sitting in, the timetable then ran as follows: in May 1970 Plessey began to employ people in the factory, setting on 30 workers; by August they had taken over its machine shop and work bay, and engaged 200 of the former employees of the Royal Naval Torpedo Factory. In January 1971 their takeover was complete.[1] The plant had been transferred to them for what the workers called a "knockdown" price of £650,000. (It was variously valued, by the workers themselves at £6m, by a spokesman of the Scottish National Party at up to £12m, and by trade union spokesmen at figures between these limits.)[2]

The workers' broadsheet described the new Plessey regime disdainfully:

> "1,000 workers were to have security immediately. And with gigantic orders scheduled for Alexandria, another 1,000 jobs would be saved. But within weeks of starting work for Plessey, the men and women found the position was completely different. Organisation was poor. There was no definite tooling programme. A lot of time was spent waiting around. Communications were non-existent — surprising for a company of Plessey's standing. There were no planning and progress departments. The workers began to smell a rat.
>
> Shop stewards tried to get Plessey to talk about these fears. The stock answer was 'things will work themselves out eventually'. Management ducked important issues (e.g. would the Mark 24 torpedo be built at the plant?). Trade union fears grew to grave concern when the company dismantled a modern machine shop suitable for up-to-date production methods. The company said their plan was to reorganise and modernise parts of the factory. Tiled floors, low roofs, air conditioning was to be put in. The unions accepted this in good faith. But the situation worsened. The unions asked for assurances on the future of the factory. They were told 'everything will sort itself out in time'. Then shop stewards noticed visitors being shown around. They were shocked to find these visitors were machine buyers.
>
> Plessey had been caught in the act. They admitted their plan to sell off machinery. But they said it was only old machinery involved. But shop stewards found brand new, valuable machinery was coming under the eye of the buyers. Again the trade unions asked for a statement on the factory's future. At this point Plessey stated their complete turnabout. First, they said, a high level decision was to be made. This would be announced shortly. Ominously, Plessey halted recruiting for the factory. They said they were

going through a difficult period. There was a recession in the machine tool trade. An announcement would be made shortly . . . Then on May 18th came the bombshell: Closure and mass sacking. Promises were made about a part of the factory being kept going to employ a few people. The workers frankly refused to believe the company any more."

The shop stewards contemplated strike action, only to rule it out as obviously irrelevant in the circumstances. Meanwhile, in June, the controversy about the Upper Clyde broke into the headlines and at the end of July, UCS had been "taken over" by its workpeople, so that a whole new style of resistance presented itself as an option, not only to the stewards, who had considered the possibility of a sit-in even before events at UCS came to a head, but also to the majority of the workers. On September 3rd, the crunch came: 250 manual workers were dismissed. *The Occupation News* reported the outcome into graphic terms:

> "The workers had a choice: accept the sack and see their factory dismantled, or take over themselves . . .
>
> They were told to report to the works gate where they had to collect their wages and cards. They were to leave in an ordinary fashion . . .
>
> It was the crucial moment. Shop stewards acted quickly.
>
> They lined the gates, asking everyone to attend a mass meeting. They laid it on the line to the workers: give in meekly, stand by as Plessey dismantled and sold the machinery; or fight: occupy the factory. The meeting voted 100% to occupy. The workers marched to the front gates, took the keys, asked the security police to leave and locked the gates. One man took the Plessey flag down from the flagpole. Then the management were served notice to quit. Since the take-over, not a scrap of machinery has been taken from the factory. Plessey has tried to smuggle components out in private cars. All cars from the factory are searched. Only a handful of the Plessey bosses are allowed in. The men work a rota system covering 24 hours a day. They patrol the grounds. And they take turns greasing and doing maintenance work on the tools and machinery."

The convenor of stewards, Eddie McLafferty, and the chairman of the stewards' committee, Jack Green, were at pains to insist during the following months that they were not particularly experienced trade union representatives.[3] Be that as it may, they made up in initiative for what they lacked in formal training. They certainly needed initiative, simply in order to communicate what was happening to the wider Labour Movement. From the beginning the press was, in general, unhelpful, and coverage was reluctant and scant. But the logistics of the occupation had first to be worked out if the men were to be able to remain in action for long enough to attract the publicity without which they had no hope of winning. The first thing the stewards did upon seizing control of the plant was to change all the locks and appoint a gateman, to whom they whimsically referred as "the key man". Hugh Inglis, who henceforward put in a steady twelve-hour day on this duty, was the controller of all entry to and exit from the plant, and maintained the strictest vigilance, checking the credentials of all who sought admission.[4] Two hundred workers joined the occupation at the beginning, while others, including a local Labour Councillor, "rejoined" it subsequently, because they had been made redundant earlier on in the year. The fact that both the local District Council and the Dumbarton Council subsequently expressed support for the occupation was important to the workers' relations with the police, who had to make some difficult judgements about what to do to enforce the rather ambiguous Scottish law of trespass.

> "We had thought" Jack Green told the Glasgow socialist newspaper *The Word* soon after the sit-in had established itself "that even a handful of men, 30-40, could take the gates and hold them. On September 3rd we asked all the men to support a takeover of the gates; they had just received their ex-gratia payments. We allowed all those who didn't want to, to leave. In fact everybody agreed to take part in the takeover of the gate, removing the management and the police, and then locking the gate, and then some left one by one. Then the following day many came back in, especially men you wouldn't expect, older men or those who opposed the decision originally. we have 150-200 regulars now."

The conditions under which the shifts in occupation worked were austere:

"a pot of tea, biscuits and two heaters were almost the only 'home comforts'. For most of the lads on the 'night shift' of the rota-based picket duty luxury is confined to a sleeping bag kept off the floor by inadequate looking layers of foam rubber. Anyone commanding one of the two camp beds is living at the 'Hilton'."[5]

The local community rallied round, however, and volunteers from among the women came in to help cook food, some of which were donated by local shopkeepers, one of whom was so helpful that the workers made him an "honorary shop steward".[6] Otherwise, the cooking was done by Alex Gallacher who learned the art of austerity victualling in a PoW camp during the Second World War.[7]

The surrounds of the factory were placarded by dozens of posters, one of which announced that the premises were "under new management". There was also a Union Jack. An attempt to run up a red flag was vetoed by 50 of the men who said they would leave if it were to be flown.[8] And so the sit-in passed from its first, to its second, to its third month . . . By Christmas, the quarter-masters of the occupation were so well organised that they celebrated their 16th week "inside" with a full Christmas dinner, including turkey and trimmings.[9] The gatehouse commisariat was covered with cards from well wishers, and the night duty pickets were "first footed" for the new year by a group of local citizens and councillors led by a couple of pipers.

The cumulative effect of all these efforts to secure and stabilise the occupation was that the journalists began to arrive, first in single spies and then in whole battalions.

At the beginning it had not been easy at all. As Eddie McLafferty told *The Word*:

> "We're disappointed with the press. They're playing us down. For instance, the *Daily Record*, only 2-3 lines. There's something wrong: maybe it's a combined decision. The local press covered us, but wouldn't support. *The Express* covered us with a hostile editorial. The people who have given coverage are *The Workers Press, Socialist Worker, The Red Mole,* the *Militant*. But not the *Morning Star*, and we're pretty disappointed about that. A coun-

cillor here contacted them and told them we would talk to them, but they haven't been."[10]

But by October the predominantly Scottish coverage had given place to serious articles in the heavy Sunday papers in London, and persistent reportage in *The Times, The Financial Times* and *The Morning Star*, which provided a great deal of information on the sit-in when Arthur Milligan's most useful articles began to appear. By November the television companies had registered their interest. In late November BBC2 screened a special feature on the occupation, and later there was a television confrontation between Eddie McLafferty and Lord Kearton of Courtaulds. By the new year all this coverage was beginning to tell, and at the beginning of January 1972 both Eddie McLafferty and Jack Green were voyaging to Cardiff to join spokesmen of UCS and the stewards of Allis Chalmers of Mold (who had just begun yet another sit-in), in a BBC Wales TV presentation on the whole question of occupations.

None of this was encouraging to Plessey's directorate. As the *Sunday Times* correspondent reported, quite early in the campaign, the management was "clearly embarrassed by the whole thing, which is why it is keeping quiet".[11]

The more that the Dumbartonshire stewards demanded a public enquiry, the less, it seems, was anyone at Plessey's willing to say. As politicians began to join the campaign, so the pressure mounted. The Scottish Nationalists committed themselves in mid-November, and twelve days later, on November 26th, ten Scottish Labour parliamentarians, led by Mr Bruce Millan, were shown round the works by Eddie McLafferty. By this time the number of workers in occupation seems to have steadied out at 84. They were heartened by the subsequent ventilation their cause received in Parliamentary questions and public statements. But the company could hardly draw comfort from it. As the sit-in continued, other Plessey workers in other parts of the country began to feel themselves involved. The problem of redundancy was one which caused anxiety throughout the whole Plessey labour-force, which numbered some 80,000; for if the recession had hit numerically controlled machine tools hard enough to scramble the Alexandria development plans, assuming these to have been realistic in the first place, then its fall-out might well affect other people within the combine. Early in October the shop stewards' works committee at Plessey's Beeston, Nottingham, plant convened a special conference in Manchester to consider policy towards closures and redundancies, and to co-ordinate the efforts of the trade union movement throughout all the Plessey factories. delegates from Swindon, Liverpool, Ilford and Scotland attended the gathering.[12] Ilford, the company's torpedo factory, blacked everything from the Argyle works.

With the threat of increasing internal pressure from labour in its other plants beginning to crystallise, and a mounting demand for a public investigation and report on the circumstances of the acquisition of the Argyle works, throughout November the Company maintained silence. "Plessey last night declined any comment" ended various press reports on the issue. But at some point during that month, it became generally known that the company

> "are now offering the factory on the market for £650,000 which the campaign organisers believe was the price paid by Plessey in 1970. They point out, however, that valuable tools and equipment have been transferred to Ilford in the meantime."[13]

This offer was conditionally welcomed as a victory by the workers. Within a month, Plessey's had found a potential partner in the Lyon Group, which sought to convert the 20 acre factory into an industrial estate. A joint company between Lyons and Plessey's was proposed, which would buy out the plant and its contents. After long and complex negotiations, the occupation of Plessey's Alexandria plant came to an end on 28 January 1972. Agreement was announced by Mr Ian McKee, the AUEW district secretary, who had played a key role in all the talks, representing his members in the sit-in: half a million square feet of floor space were to be divided between several industrial companies and tenants, and with the first such tenant would move in within a month, to provide 70 jobs immediately. "The proposals" said Mr McKee "have been accepted unanimously".[14] On 7 February, the 70 survivors of the sit-in started work, preparing machinery for the new incumbants, and on that day they handed over the keys to the new Lyon-Plessey Consortium.[15] But this was not simply a change of employment. It was a victory. As Eddie McLafferty explained to a conference of the Institute of Workers' Control:

> "In the past in Alexandria throughout all the closures and redundancies the men have maintained a kind of passive outlook on the situation. In the usual situation you have maybe about two days strike, you have two or three meetings with the full time officials, you meet the company, you meet your MPs, and at the end of the day you just have to go back and negotiate terms. We realise we may be defeated (although defeat is a word that, up to now, the members haven't really considered at all). But we've got to be realists in a situation like this. We could go on in occupation for quite some time with nothing happening at all, but even then it will have been worthwhile. I can tell you for a fact that in the last redundancy I was in in Alexandria, I walked out of the gate. We took no action. I walked out of the gate at night with my cards in my pocket, down to the Labour Exchange with my head buried and my tail between my legs. But this time, if we are defeated, whether after 17 weeks occupation or after a year's occupation, then we'll walk down Alexandria with our heads held high in the air."[16]

Not only did the Plessey men have reason to hold up their heads: this example was to help transform the possibilities of resistance to many tens of thousands of other victims of redundancy and closure, and within a very short time at that.

Sit-in in Wales

Mold is a small market town in Flintshire, with a population of some 8,000, very far indeed from the Vale of Leven, leave alone the sullen streets of Clydeside.

Employment opportunities there have hinged on the nearby Steelworks in Shotton, itself none too secure, or on the land and in the satisfaction of the complex of needs developed by farmers. Jones Balers, the firm which created the only factory in town, grew up to service some of these needs. It was a dynamic enterprise, and during the nineteen-fifties it began to sell agricultural machinery all over the world, as far afield as Japan. Its American agent was Allis Chalmers of Milwaukee. Having become indispensible as an outlet for Jones Balers, Allis Chalmers took over the Mold/Rhosemoor factory in 1961, at about the same time that they set up in their Essendene plant in Lincolnshire.

The Mold plant manufactured three dozen machines a week, and by the beginning of 1972 it was employing 120 people. Since the take-over, Allis Chalmers had concentrated all production of earth-moving equipment in the Lincolnshire factory, and all agricultural machine manufacturing in Mold. They still made Jones Balers, but some of them were sprayed a different colour, and labelled 'Allis Chalmers' for the appropriate market.[17] The British agent was F.H. Burgess, who also dealt in all Allis Chalmers spares. Burgess were associates of Bamford Agricultural Engineering, a firm based in Uttoxeter. In 1971 Bamfords took over Allis Chalmers, almost certainly with the intention simply of acquiring the licence to make Jones Balers. The Mold factory, which was organised by the Amalgamated Union of Engineering Workers, was apparently to be phased out. The takeovers took place on October 1st 1971, and the union was partially informed of what had happened on October 4th. At this time the men were told that Bamfords would make balers in Uttoxeter, increasing their output to 180 a week.[18] Immediately demonstrations were organised, which gathered a lot of support in the town, but a negligible press outside it. Their MP, Sir Arthur Myers, flew in and gave them a ten minute interview ("including introductions and farewells").[19] Apart from that and a lot of concerned assistance from activists of Plaid Cymru, the Welsh National Party, who sought out alternative purchasers for the factory in the hope of keeping it open, nothing much happened until New Year's Eve, when the men were given their notice. At the same time, the union was informed that there would be an opportunity for a meeting with management on January 2nd 1972.

Hugh Hughes, the convenor, told reporters from the *Red Mole* that this encounter was "a farce":

> "Management had not been briefed on the situation, nor did they have the power to take decisions, instead they told the workers, who were still carrying on as usual, to dismantle the factory machines for transportation to the Uttoxeter plant."[20]

So the factory was taken over on January 3rd. "We will stay in until management begins meaningful negotiations" said Mr Hughes.[21] After preliminary plans had been agreed by the shop stewards the day before, a meeting of all workers, both manual and whitecollar groups, unanimously accepted the proposal to sit in. They organised a rota of three hourly shifts to maintain 24-hour occupation, and then a workshop for preparing placards saying "Save Allis Chalmers" and "We Demand the Right to Work in Wales". These were distributed throughout the township and eagerly displayed in local shops. Apart from the short-shift innovation, the sit-in had many features in common with that at Alexandria, although no prior consultation had taken place between the two groups of workers about it. The Mold workers, like those at the Argyle works, invited management to station their own security men with the occupying force, in order to cover themselves against possible charges of pilfering. At the same time, they forbade the movement of either machinery or stocks, which meant that they had instantly established a tourniquet on the supply of spares: a question which could assume great importance as a bargaining lever in the event of a prolonged occupation.

Appeals to the other Allis-Chalmers factory at

Essendene for support were apparently ineffective, at least in part because of the weakness of union representation in that plant. Few appeals seem to have been made to any other groups of workers. The Alexandria workers travelled down to meet the Mold men's spokesmen when they took part in a Welsh TV programme.[22] Apart from that the negotiations which the occupation made necessary for Bamfords took place over in Leicestershire, and involved the officers of the AUEW. That seems to have been the sum total of the involvement of Rhosemoor men outside their own immediate area. There was a considerable suspicion of political connections of any kind whatever. A young worker there told *Seven Days*, the short-lived socialist photo-weekly, that by acting as they had they had put themselves at the centre of initiative:

> "We are on the job; we can decide for ourselves. What goes on at Westminster? Somebody gets up 'There's a sit-in at Mold — they want support'. He's asked. He's mentioned it in the House. But that's all. Nobody is going to reply 'right, we're going to support them' . . . *We* can carry out what we say. Politicians can't."[23]

If this shows a certain syndicalist spirit, it should not be interpreted in any directly insurrectionary sense. Hugh Hughes gave an interview to the *Sunday Times*, in which he was quoted as saying "Workers' Control? I've got enough bloody problems already!"[24] The ambiguities in the situation were further complicated by the photograph which the newspaper published at the same time, showing Mr Hughes (whom it described as a "special constable from the local police station") standing sentry over the entrance to the factory whose occupation he had at least partly organised and led.

The Mold occupation was shortlived, and it ended in victory. From the beginning it was clear that local community support was almost complete, and the result was that various offers were made to buy the factory. For instance, a supermarket proprietor from Prestatyn came over with an offer of 100 jobs if he could move in.[25] But Bamfords themselves, who were not, it seems, in any degree the object of illwill from the Rhosemoor workers, had not by then worked out their own plans for the future of the factory. On 18 January, after 16 days of sit-in, a settlement was reached, maintaining employment for all workers for at least three months, and guaranteeing at least 80 jobs thereafter. As it turned out, the Mold factory did not contract, but expanded, after this initial reprieve had expired.

The Fisher-Bendix Occupation

Two days after special constable Hughes led his men into the occupation of the factory at Mold, workers took over yet another plant. This one was in solid trade union country, at Kirkby, near Liverpool. Not only was it part of the legendary labour movement of Merseyside, but it was also, at that time, part of the parliamentary constituency of Harold Wilson; the old Huyton division.

The Fisher-Bendix occupation was, from its inception, a model of efficient trade union organisation. Perhaps the fact that the national press was getting used to sit-ins may explain why it was not far more extensively reported than was in fact the case: for, during its first phase, every day it developed some exemplary new initiative. It began with a bang, and it went on that way until the Leader of the Opposition intervened in order to produce a solution. *The Financial Times* reported the first day with all its characteristic coolness:

> "Workers at the Fisher-Bendix domestic appliances factory at Kirkby (Lancs) 'took over' yesterday after the company decided to go ahead with a closure plan. Nearly 1,000 employees — who had collected £2,500 in a special fighting fund — asked the management to leave after talks to break the deadlock had failed. The management left, but scores of white-collar workers decided to join the take-over. While the talks were being held in the Boardroom 200 workers walked in and staged a noisy demonstration. Mr Tom Staples, shop stewards' spokesman, said: 'We are continuing to allow materials to be delivered to the factory, but no work is being done here.
>
> 'Unemployment in Kirkby is already very high, and we are simply not prepared to sit back and watch another 1,000 men and

women be thrown into the dole queue. The take-over will last as long as it is needed'."[26]

The act of dismissing the management has been variously described. One participant recalled it two years later, at the beginning of the second Kirkby sit-in[27] "while management were telling our stewards we were all sacked, we invaded the boardroom, secured all the keys and gave the management five minutes to get off the premises. The mass-meeting that followed was the most electrifying, exciting and stimulating experience anyone can imagine".[28] *The Morning Star* gave an account which confirmed that 200 workers had invaded the boardroom, while 400 demonstrated outside.

> "Mr Jack Spriggs, the engineering union convenor, then informed the management that the factory had been taken over, and the workers were in possession of the keys. After a break, talks were resumed at 1.00 pm but all the management offered was a 26-day recess to allow for further talks. After rejecting this, the stewards told the management to leave the factory and informed them that they would not be allowed in again. The workers then set up their own security arrangement at the factory gate . . ."[29]

These arrangements consisted of a round-the-clock manning rota, just as in the other occupied plants: but as an aid to security, the men also welded the main gates of the factory together, in a sort of informal ceremony. Jack Spriggs then informed the press:

> "We have taken over the factory. Nothing will be allowed to move out, but we will allow deliveries into the premises. We will continue the occupation until something is done about protecting jobs of all people employed here."[30]

By the following day, the occupation was secure. Women joined with the men in the sit-in on all shifts except the nightshift. "As the workers arrive to take their places they are signed in by the workers' own security guards at the gates" reported the *Morning Star*:[31] "A group of workers today went to the Moorgate Road depot — the firm's servicing and spares base for the entire country — and loaded the stock of spares on to lorries and drove them to the factory. Works convenor Mr

Jack Spriggs said: 'We will now be able to stop the entire servicing operation throughout the country. We now control the factory equipment worth about £1 million and thousands of pounds worth of spares. We also control a vast amount of finished equipment and are in a very strong position'." All this was quickly understood by Thorn Electrical Industries, the owners of the plant, who informed *The Times* that "we very much regret that this action by employees is compelling Fisher-Bendix to take appropriate steps to protect its interests".[32] At the same time, a spokesman of the company denied that its servicing operations would be seriously impeded, insisting that the Moorgate Road depot was "only one of many controlled by the company".

The stewards had clearly thought out their strategy in very good detail, and had carefully studied the experience of both UCS and Plessey Alexandria.[33] At the same time, they knew their own local trade union movement was utterly dependable provided only that they were able to convince it of the justification for extended solidarity action. So they put a considerable effort into explaining the background to the dispute, in order to mobilise the widest possible support. Jack Spriggs is a talented communicator, and he was able to put his story across in a compelling manner. It would be difficult to improve upon his account of the troubled history of the plant, as reported, virtually verbatim, in *Seven Days*, whose correspondents attended a mass meeting in the factory soon after the start of the occupation (this meeting comprised not only the workers, but their families. Girl friends and wives were specifically invited, and their enthusiastic support was clearly a crucial factor in maintaining the workpeople's morale). This is what Jack Spriggs had to say:

> "There's a long history of bad management in this establishment. We were originally opened, at a cost of £3.5 million, from the British Motor Corporation. BMC got huge Government grants to build and open this factory. And over a period of years they've

been continually going to the Board of Trade for more development grants because this particular factory is in a depressed area. Over a period of time, it's been a stamping ground for people just to go down to sit in the Boardroom drinking scotch and not care what happens in the factory.

There have been continuous changes of managers. Over the years we've had no less than 12 managers, we're on our thirteenth at the moment, and each and every one of them has either not had the ability, or has not been allowed to use his ability, to make this factory tick. The wages in this establishment have come from a measly pittance of something like £11 a week on a three shift system 10 years to about £28 a week now. This has all been done by the efforts of the workers and their skilled negotiators . . . The wages in this factory under a day-wage measurement system, producing x amount of components in x amount of time, and then when Parkinson-Cowan slid into the piece we changed to a system of payment for productivity.

Unfortunately productivity deals up and down the country have created unemployment. But at that time everybody was feeling that if they were producing more goods they would be getting more money. So the workers in this factory boosted their personal output by 50% . . . And we were brought along nicely, listening to the overtures that management were putting out: that we were expanding, producing more washing machines, steel sinks, radiators, gas fires and gas cookers. Suddenly we found they were going to discontinue the tumble driers. That was 18 months ago. They brought in a small gas cooker, and some fires, and the manager said at that time that what he was going to do was introduce a new cooker which would be able to take more people on and make more work for people already in the establishment. That was the last we would see of the electric tumble drier. It was going completely out of business in the UK and everywhere.

The management sent for us again and said 'We're losing a million pounds', so we said 'Where are you losing this million pounds?' They refused the evidence to us that we at Fisher-Bendix in Kirkby were responsible for the loss . . . They decided then to do away with the stainless sink programme. And we said, 'But you're not doing away with the sink. You're transferring this work to a firm in Scotland'. They said we were over subscribed. And so the situation went along and people left. At one time we had 2,200 people and now we find ourselves with something like 900.

June 1 last year, one week after Thorn Electric had bought the factory on May 24, the shop stewards were sent for by the company. And while we went upstairs there were all kinds of superintendents down below with pocketfuls of paper. As the stewards were going upstairs to speak to the management the superintendents were giving out pieces of paper on the shop floor which said that they were going to sack 500 people; more than half of the labour force. We said 'What's happened to negotiation. What's happened to the courtesy of procedure?' They said that as far as they were concerned the union had no say in the matter, for this was the way it was going to be. We told them that wasn't the way it was going to be. They said they were going to discontinue the washing machines.

We had a mass demonstration and went and met Harold Wilson at the Labour Club. And we also employed every possible channel in the trade union movement. The company completely ignored the trade unions, to such a degree that some weeks after the announcement the people in this factory went on strike. It was quickly recognised by the unions concerned and we fought a nine-weeks battle . . . The dockers stepped in and blacked all Thorn's goods. What a change came over Sir Jules Thorn. He sent a message down that he was prepared to reinstate all the workpeople immediately."

At this point the stewards, having won their battle, were willing to accept what they called 'normalisation', and to work through the duly constituted procedures for the reprieve they needed.

"We contacted Harold Wilson and the Merseyside MPs and we also contacted the trade unions. We also got ample evidence, sheets and sheets of paper that had been dug out, to show that the work was in fact not being taken off the market but had in fact been transferred to Spain. The electric tumble drier was about to be imported into this country in June of last year. There was also evidence that it had been planned to manufacture the washing machine in Spain. And that's when the workers said 'You're not on'. They decided that nothing connected with the washing machine would go out of this factory. So there was some time of argie-bargie about movement of tools.

We adopted deliberate delaying tactics to give MPs and the trade unions enough time to sift and analyse all the evidence that we produced for them. But the company said they would not have these tactics much longer. On 8th December they called a meeting and at that meeting Mr Sidney, who represents Thorn's, said the reason he wanted to transfer the work to Newcastle was because of the economic situation. They felt a moral obligation to a depressed area like Newcastle. We feel very sympathetic towards the workers of Newcastle. But we are not going to give our wages away and go on the dole queue. 'Mr Sidney' I said, 'the reason you're transferring the work to Newcastle is to create bigger profits for Sir Jules Thorn and his massive empire, and don't you deny it' — and he didn't. There's no big boss interested in the welfare of the people. What you gain, what you get, you work hard for. It's my considered opinion there was a lot of nonsense spoken that day and very little evidence put forward.

We continued to argue through normal channels, that an acute situation had developed at the factory. They offered a few more extra pence. They offered a few more extra pounds. Who was doing the panicking? Them or us? We never asked for money, we asked for a job.

Then they said that on January 3rd, they were going to dismantle the machines, come what may.

We went away for our Christmas break and said we'd worry about that on January 3rd. January arrived and the company told us that we'd lost the 12 managers. Sacked or left: we couldn't care less. We treated it as a non-event, because that's what managers are in this factory — non-events.

And we come to the point. We asked management, 'What are you going to do about this factory machinery?' They said they were going to carry out their procedure. Monday went by, Tuesday arrived and they instructed the chief engineer to tell individual fitters and mates, electricians and anybody else, to dismantle the machinery. They told the chief engineer at that time that if they refused to carry out this lawful demand, he must sack the workers. We replied: 'If he attempts to sack any more of our members we will have no doubt as to what our action will be'."

At this point, Jack Spriggs was obviously eyeball to eyeball with the management spokesman, Mr Brashaw. It was Mr Brashaw who blinked. Asked if intended to carry out his threat to sack those who declined the order to dismantle, he said he did. Whereupon the convenor told him, "The best thing you can do is get your coat on and leave these premises. When you're out of the way, you can do no harm". *Seven Days* continues the shop stewards' narrative:

> "He immediately panicked and got in touch with London. Mr Sidney Carns said 'Ask the boys to wait 24 hours and I'll come down and have a chat with them'. So we said, fine, try to keep the thing moving democratically — we waited 24 hours. We told them the feelings of the people in this factory; and they did not believe us. Not until 200 people invaded the boardroom and then I've never seen such scared people in my life. In fact on the way out a councillor was coming up to meet Mr Carns by previous arrangement, he offered him a white flag of truce so he could get back

and have some discussions.

Then the company's attitude eased a little. When I say eased, shall I say some of the process eased a little? They agreed that they would have a 28-day stay of execution — as they termed it — while other people got involved. The workers of this factory could not accept that any longer. We'd been living on a knife-edge. For those of you who don't work here it's hard to imagine the way these people here, over the last six months, have not known what's going to happen next . . . They couldn't stand it any longer."[34]

Once the plant was occupied, the dossier on the company's alleged equivocation was greatly fattened up once the workers found their way around the abandoned filing system. At the Newcastle-upon-Tyne Conference on work-ins and sit-ins which was convened by the Institute for Workers' Control early in January 1972, the Fisher-Bendix delegate reported:

> "The new management told us that the place was not viable, because they said there were no sales for their products. Yet we came across contracts — 5 contracts — stating that our main customer, Potterton, had placed orders with Fisher-Bendix to the tune of a million radiators or more, orders which could carry us up to 1974 and after. We also found contracts which dealt with the removal of the transfer of the washing machine business from Kirkby to Spain. We were told by the company that this washing machine business was finished altogether. Obviously this was not so. The same is true for the Fisher Low sinks, the stainless steel sinks. The truth about the sinks was this: our maintenance people spent six months early last year laying out the plant, a lot of it new plant, ready for the production of the sinks, but during the same week that this layout was completed, the management sent orders down for the plant to be dismantled and moved elsewhere.[35]

Soon afterwards Jack Spriggs expanded on this theme at a mass-meeting in the factory:

> "When you look at a couple of letters that have been put out these last few days, you'll see — Brothers, colleagues, sisters, visitors — why we had to take this action. One letter is from Parkinson-Cowan Services and it states:
>
> 'Dear Business Customer,
>
> It has been reluctantly decided to cease the manufacture of Bendix washing machines at the factory at Kirkby on 16th July 1971. This is due to heavy overheads and higher production costs'.

It goes on to say in an interesting part
> 'This does not mean the departure of Bendix from the washing machine scene. Bendix products will continue to be marketed and the range will be expanded. In fact another product shortly to be added is a new line in domestic electric tumble-driers'.

That was ours. That's the one we built here. It's now being produced in Carsa of Madrid. And another one. September 23, 1971. From Thorn Electric to Mr Ellis, Fisher-Bendix, Kirkby.
> 'Mr Ellis, I am glad I have had the opportunity of speaking to you . . . when you were in my office. I look forward to our meeting, in the meantime . . . I also hear that two additional washing machines are likely to go into circulation in the near future'.

Two additional washing machines — there weren't to be any Bendix washing machines. Lies upon lies, deceit upon deceit. If we stood for it here and the trade union movement stood for it, then you've got to move back, not 20 years, but 100 years of time."[36]

Whilst they outlined their indictment of the company, the shop stewards were rapidly consolidating their support in the trade union movement. Immediately the occupation took place, messages of support began to flow in from all over the country, but the initial effort of the stewards was naturally concentrated on securing their home base on Merseyside. Simon Fraser, the secretary of Liverpool Trades Council, quickly arranged for a meeting of trade unions and shop stewards throughout his region, to hear the spokesman of the Fisher-Bendix workers.[37] The Liverpool District Committee of the AUEW called for a one-day solidarity strike.[38] Dockers in Liverpool began discussions on 8th January, and agreed to black Thorn goods at once. By the following weekend they had persuaded the National Port Shop Steward's Conference to recommend similar action and to appeal for financial support.[39] The Chairman of Kirkby town council addressed a rally in the factory, and told the workers:

> "I am absolutely delighted that you are not going to lie down and accept redundancy, but are prepared to do something practical to fight against unemployment."[40]

Eric Heffer, together with two other Labour MPs, attended a subsequent mass-meeting and said that:

> "the working-class movement is stronger, better organised and more confident than in the 1930s. Mr Heath can forget if he thinks he can grind the workers' noses in the dust."[41]

Jack Spriggs had an hour-long interview with Harold Wilson to discuss the closure, and this began a strenuous intervention in the case by the Leader of the Opposition. Within a couple of weeks they were both engaged in talks in London, and by the end of the month Mr Wilson was taking the chair at meetings between the stewards and the company's representatives, leading directly to the ensuing settlement.[42]

Meantime, the plans for a one-day strike on Merseyside went ahead, and the AUEW proposal was taken up by the Trades Council and the dockers, who were already considering a stoppage in protest against the level of unemployment in the Liverpool area. In the outcome, a joint stoppage was organised for Wednesday, 26th January.

Trade unionists were not the only supporters to rally to the Fisher-Bendix banner ("Under New Management", it read boldly, outside the factory). The Everyman Theatre Company put on excerpts from John McGrath's rock-musical "Soft or a Girl" in the canteen. *The Liverpool Free Press* published special numbers on the occupation. The Scaffold, The Spinners, Adrian Henri and various pop-groups gave concerts and readings. Cinema Action and CAST made the pilgrimage from London and were cordially received. Arthur Dooley, the sculptor, mounted a special exhibition:

> "In the post show-rooms of the Fisher-Bendix office block the Dooley exhibition includes a significant piece of sculpture which typifies the present mood here and elsewhere in the country. It is a crucifix, but Christ has come down from the cross in a gesture which says, 'We have had enough. You will not crucify us any more'."[43]

The Liverpool Free School visited the factory. One of

the children was reported as saying:

> "Now you've got the factory. Why don't you keep it? Why let the managers take over again?"[44]

The same preconception was echoed by others. While the direct support for the occupation was widespread, and its impact upon the independent socialist groupings was dramatic, the immediate solution to the dispute had to be negotiated within the given order of things. Mr Wilson's talks were not about the evolution of a new order of self-management, but about the conditions under which employment could be maintained. In this sense, the sit-in, although it was a different tactic, had the same fundamental limits as the work-in at UCS. Many socialist activists did not find this comfortable. For example, the anarcho-socialist grouping which publishes *Solidarity*, a mimeographed journal which is written in a sparklingly direct, not to say uncompromising, language, had, from the beginning of the Plessey sit-in, distinguished it most sharply from the work-in at UCS.[45] Of sit-ins it approved, because it thought they maintained an unambiguously contestatory style. Of work-ins it most definitely disapproved, because they seemed to be compromised with the productive orientations (or Calvinist work-ethics) of capitalist society. So *Solidarity* was positively ecstatic about the Fisher-Bendix experience. It published a most useful descriptive pamphlet on the events of the occupation, in which one of its co-authors wrote:

> "The actions of the workers at Fisher-Bendix has reaffirmed many of our ideas. But they are doing something more. They are teaching us how these ideas can be made a reality. The lessons learnt in such struggles far exceed anything that might come out of discussion alone. In giving the Kirkby workers all our support, and asking others to do likewise, we should also take from them what they have to offer: a living example of courage, initiative, plain common-sense in handling their affairs, and a lesson in self-management."[46]

Yet, at the same time, the Trotskyist journal *The Red Mole* was warning:

"Factory occupation is a sharper weapon against the bosses' economic attack . . . But without the new industrial front being linked by militants to a new political strategy, posing a revolutionary alternative, it will fail. It will fail because these industrial actions create a political vacuum which will be filled by the Labour Party. Thus Wedgwood Benn can make UCS a platform for his politics, and Fisher-Bendix is also being used by Merseyside Labour MPs . . . The pattern is being set for the most advanced workers to continue the see-saw between total reliance on industrial action (syndicalism) and political reliance on the Labour Party. The only alternative, however small, is the revolutionary left."[47]

What both these journals ignored, however, was one very simple truism: if the condition of the British political economy is such that workpeople are compelled to challenge the authority of industrial management in a thoroughgoing manner, then those same conditions can transform the structure of their own organisations. Why Jack Spriggs should reject the help of Labour MPs, or refuse the good offices of their leaders, was never explained by his critics. It could not be explained in terms of the interests of the people he represented, without entering the field of "revolutionary" mysticism. In reality, the approach to self-management lay not around, but through, the structures of the Labour Movement, which had been created by previous generations of workers to defend their interests and which would never be abandoned while there was the slightest hope that they could be reclaimed for their original purposes. The audacious initiatives of Tony Benn, and the rapid shift of opinion in both the official union machines and the National Organisation of the Labour party, had, by 1972, made such hope not only plausible, but positively compelling, to the shop stewards of Fisher-Bendix no less than the workers who elected them. And in the short run, these hopes seemed to have been borne out when the Wilson intervention rescued the jobs of 730 people, and the *Financial Times* could report:

"The jobs of 730 Fisher-Bendix workers, who in January occupied their Kirkby, Liverpool, factory for three weeks when they heard they were to be made redundant, have been saved. The Thorn Electrical Industries' subsidiary which manufactures radiators and night storage heaters, originally proposed to close down operations at Kirkby this month. Yesterday, however, it announced that agreement had been reached for a newly-formed consortium called International Property Development to take over manufacturing operations there at the end of this month. A statement from Fisher-Bendix last night said the move would provide continuity of employment for the workforce at the plant and 'enhance opportunities in the future'. The decision was warmly welcomed by union representatives at the factory who described it as 'a complete victory'."[48]

It *was* another victory. That more battles were in prospect, few would have denied. But it was a victory, nevertheless.

Footnotes

1. *Plessey Occupation News* published by the Occupying Works Committee, undated, sometime after November 1971.
2. The workers' estimate was given in *Occupation News*, above, Mr William Lindsay, chairman of the Glasgow Regional Council of the SNP, in denouncing the terms of the Plessey acquisition, and calling for a public enquiry, advanced the £12m estimate as "possible" (see *The Scotsman* 15 November 1971). John Fryer, in the *Sunday Times* of 10 October 1971 pointed out that £1½m had been spent on one section of the building alone, as recently as 1968. Arthur Milligan, in the *Morning Star* 29 October 1971, gave an estimate of £7m for the whole works, and wrote:
    > "One unique, dustfree unit was worth £1½m, and a pile of stock material would fetch almost half the amount paid for the whole place."
3. *The Red Mole* Interview from *The Word* of Glasgow, reprinted, 20 October 1971.
4. *Morning Star* Report by Arthur Milligan 10 December 1971.
5. *Morning Star* 29 October 1971.
6. *Sunday Times* 10 October 1971.
7. *The Times* 29 November 1971.
8. *Red Mole* 20 October 1971.
9. *The Times & The Morning Star* 24 December 1971.
10. *Red Mole* 20 October 1971.
11. *Sunday Times* 10 October 1971.
12. *Financial Times* 6 October 1971.
13. *Scotsman* 15 November 1971. The demand made by the chairman of the Association of Scottish Nationalist Trade Unionists, Mr William Johnston, that "the degree to which Plessey had depleted the Alexandria Works" should be investigated was echoed in Parliament by Mr

Dick Douglas, the Labour MP for Clackmannan, at the beginning of December. See the *Glasgow Herald*, 3 December 1971.
14. *Times* 29 January 1972.
15. *Glasgow Herald* 8 February 1972.
16. Speech to the Conference on Work-ins and Sit-ins organised by the IWC at Newcastle University on January 8th-9th 1972.
17. Inside Occupied Mold: *Seven Days* January 1972.
18. *The Red Mole* 24 January 1972.
19. *Seven Days, ibid.*
20. *The Red Mole, ibid.*
21. *Morning Star* 4 January 1972. The reports in the London daily papers are conflicting on the numbers involved in the sit-in. *The Morning Star* consistently reports that 140 people were involved. *The Times* reported that 180 were sitting in and quoted Mr Hughes as saying that "the entire labour force was 100% behind the occupation" (150% to be exact). Later the *Guardian* had the number of jobs at stake represented as 200 (8 January 1972). The actual number was, as *Seven Days* gave it, 120: a striking testimony to the value of 'amateur' reportage.
22. *Morning Star* 6 January 1972.
23. Brian Thomas interviewed in *Seven Days, ibid.*
24. *Sunday Times* 23 January 1972.
25. *Guardian* 9 January 1972.
26. *Financial Times* 6 January 1972. *The Guardian* gave the numbers involved as 600 (6 January 1972), while various other figures were cited elsewhere.
27. To which we shall turn later on: see below Chapter IX.
28. *Socialist Worker* 20 July 1974. An article by an AUEW member who was involved.
29. *Morning Star* 6 January 1972.
30. *The Times* 6 January 1972.
31. *Morning Star* 7 January 1972.
32. *The Times* 7 January 1972.
33. Cf. the interview with Jack Spriggs in *The Red Mole* 24 January 1972:
    Q. We understand you visited the UCS and Plesseys in preparation for this occupation. What did you learn?
    J.S. We decided that UCS-type operation of a work-in was impracticable for us. Plesseys was more effective. A work-in involves problems of supply to keep production going, sales of products and payment of workers. At Plesseys a strike-in is tying up the movement of machinery, breaking the company's contracts and causing widespread disruption — it is a more effective weapon.
34. *Seven Days* 19 January 1972.
35. From the records of the IWC Newcastle Conference on Work-ins and Sit-ins held at Newcastle University on January 8-9 1972.
36. *Seven Days, ibid.*
37. *Times* 8 January 1972.
38. *Morning Star* 8 January 1972.
39. *Morning Star* 10 January 1972.
40. *Morning Star* 8 January 1972.
41. *Financial Times* 13 January 1972.
42. *Morning Star* 12 January 1972, *The Times* 24 January 1972, *Morning*

SIT-INS

Star 29 January 1972, *Financial Times* 31 January 1972.
43. *Morning Star* 24 January 1972.
44. *Seven Days* 2 February 1972.
45. *Solidarity* Vol.6, No.5; Vol.6, No.11. *Solidarity*, like the *Socialist Worker*, the journal of the International Socialists, believed that sit-ins were justifiable as acts of resistance to capital, while work-ins were in some sense compromised by a spirit of "collaboration". This attitude was summed up in the *Solidarity* cartoon of a UCS meeting in which an improbably suave shop steward is saying: "Brothers! If the bosses won't exploit us, we'll have to do it ourselves".
46. *Under New Management* Solidarity Pamphlet 39, 25 January 1972, p.12.
47. *The Red Mole* 24 January 1972.
48. *Financial Times* 21 March 1972.

Chapter V

Working on in Sheffield: A Steel Man's Account

Failure at BSA

While the sit-ins were showing, and rather quickly at that, their capacity to gain real concessions in redundancy battles, two other work-ins were proposed during the period immediately after the UCS project got under way. One succeeded in a limited way. The other did not.

At BSA Motor Cycles, in Birmingham, mass redundancies provoked stewards to launch a whole series of proposals for resistance, from mooting a strike, through suggesting a sit-in, to canvassing support for a work-in. In the event, nothing happened.[1] Partly, no doubt, the difference between the unemployment statistics in the Midlands and in Scotland accounts for some of the reluctance of workpeople to stand fast on their right to work, even though, in Birmingham at the time, the dole queues were unhealthily long compared with anything known in that city in recent decades. But we are bound to wonder whether this collapse of resistance was not also partly due to a sense of the difficulties involved. Like the GEC workers in Liverpool, the Birmingham men were contemplating a work-in at a mass-production enterprise, engaged in processing numerous components into a large number of units of produce for a mass market. The whole problem of supplies and co-ordination, and of sales, became too vast to contemplate. To supply a motor-cycle factory with components and materials is to need to master hundreds of vital connections with other sales outlets. Many relatively costly units of production, mass-produced, with a short time involved in manufacturing each: these are not good conditions for "working-in".

Some of these problems were in fact partially surmounted in the later Briant Colour Printing work-in,[2] and, on a very different scale, at the takeover of their leather goods workshop by the women of Fakenham[3] to which we shall return. And at Triumph Meriden, actual production of motor-cycles was very competently organised in a workers' co-operative, but not on an adversary basis, during the long, necessary, preliminary sit-in. But the larger the scale of an enterprise and the more complex its product may be, the more intractable these questions are likely to prove.

Does this mean that BSA workers could do nothing? Of course not: they could have sat-in, and had they done so, they would have aroused considerable sympathy throughout the Midlands, afflicted as the surrounding counties were by uncomfortably high levels of employment. Yet, while support might have been attracted if a basis for action could have been found, in the absence of such action, nothing *would* be done.[4]

The work-on at River Don Steelworks

The second work-in to be effectively undertaken after the initiative on the Clyde was at Sheffield, at the River Don Steelworks. This was a qualified, if short-lived, victory, which offers at least one important lesson.

In the Autumn of 1971, the British Steel Corporation announced plans to close the River Don plant, in the course of "rationalisation" which, as *New Society* commented, was "a synonym for minimising competition".[5] Parts of the order book of this plant were to be ceded to a private competitor, while its unique heavy forge was simply to be shut. The work-in achieved a sharp rephasing of the redundancy schedule, but the forge was reprieved for a very unusual reason. The workers, led by representatives of staff unions, with much technical support from lower management, whose attitudes were anything but militant in the conventional sense, compiled a list of customers for heavy forgings, and approached them all with the question, did they know of BSC's plans? Since the intended closure would have meant that heavy forgings could only be obtained abroad, there was an almost instant queue of complainants at Lord Melchett's office, and the decision was revoked. The story was told at the 1972 (Newcastle) Conference of the Institute for Workers' Control by Roy Wilson, the delegate from the River Don Works Committee:

> "We set off on June 28th 1971, being told at 4.15 pm that we were going to be 'hived off', because our part of the nationalised sector was going to be given over to the private sector in exchange for a monopoly in stainless steel. If everybody had given over and accepted this proposal the whole River Don plant was to go as part of that deal, and there wouldn't have been a ripple, I'm convinced. Nobody would have said anything except 'here we go again, first we're nationalised then we're not'. Now we are, then we're not, and when Labour get in again we'll be nationalised again. But they proposed to take half, and a rather lucrative half at that, of River Don works.
>
> I ought to tell you that River Don Works, as a works, is the only place in this country capable of forging and machining units of up to 200 tons in weight. Everybody else does up to 80 tons, and as it happens, at Firth Brown's, who are less than half a mile down the road, they can do up to 80 tons, but they've not been doing very well. So they decided, as part of the deal for the acquisition of a monopoly of stainless steel, to surrender to private enterprise all our capacity up to 80 tons. We could see that there was no chance when this happened. If they were going to deprive us of all work up to 80 tons this would mean that we would have no chance with what was left, because we knew that we were already losing a certain amount of money because of the economic situation.
>
> We've complained over a great number of years that we wanted a much better melting capacity and I don't intend to get involved in that particular part of the argument. The point is that under the proposals of June 1971 we would no longer have been viable.
>
> We were told on June 28th that at the same time as the news was being broken to us, Mr Davies was announcing in Parliament that he was giving the go-ahead to this particular part of the deal. It was said that there were extensive rationalisation plans involving the drop forge and the die shop, which would be sold off as a

going concern, while the vacuum remelting and the electric slag furnaces would be removed from River Don and resited at Firth Brown. And it was claimed also that the goodwill and the order book in the department of medium forgings (up to seventy tons) would go to Allied Steels. This actually implied in practice that there was to be a transfer of 1,000 men into the private sector, while some men would be made redundant in the highly profitable special steel section, which would become a virtual monopoly for Firth Brown's. But the third thing that would have happened would have been the redundancy of up to four and a half thousand men, unless there had been very substantial investment in new plant. And we knew that that much investment in plant wasn't forthcoming in the agreement, because it was blatantly stated by the Director of Special Steels that we would have to pay our way or be terminated.

So this announcement came as a tremendous shock: because in Sheffield it was like the collapse of the Rock of Gibraltar, since everybody had always said that 'when you're in English Steel that's it, you're made'. My own particular family has over 200 years of service within that place. I was involved myself with two others who were talking to the *Sunday Times* a little while ago, and the three of us had put 80 years in between us. So you can see that we were, in a way, a set of veterans.

When we became aware of the problem, on the following day, which was Tuesday morning, at 10.30 am, the management met our full-time trade union officials. While the officials were meeting we had our first spell of trouble. Some of the full-time officials brought in their convenors and they in turn brought in various representatives of their unions, because there are twenty-seven different unions involved in this fight for the jobs of 4,500 men. But when one or two officials brought their men in, the other full-time officials said 'if he's bringing his in I want mine in' and generated a hell of a lot of trouble: so in the end they said, away with it, we'll just send the full-time officials in, and we'll conduct our own meeting. We went out and talked amongst ourselves, and on the next day, we went to London to lobby our MPs. While we were there we virtually formed the committee which is still operating right now six months later. We did all our own work going down and coming back up on the train. And when we came back we were wiser men and we had started on something big: I don't know what we really did think at the time, but we certainly knew it was going to be hard work.

I belong to a staff union, the old DATA, which is now called TASS, which sounds rather like a newsagency, but nevertheless we all got involved, as indeed all the staff unions got involved, with the manual workers, and we said, 'look we'll do this together'. This was important to the struggle for a number of reasons. First of all, the staff workers have all the inside knowledge of what can be expected from the melting shops. We were able to put a report together, in which we set out what became a famous viability survey which was certainly hammered from all sorts of areas. We pushed that report all over the show. We set out to prove to everyone that there was not only an opportunity to make the River Don Plant viable, but that we could show how it could be done.

We also said something which turned out to be more important still. We showed in our report, and we really proved our point, that if they closed us down there was no one, and I mean no one, in the United Kingdom, who was capable of producing a forging of over 80 tons or a casting of over 80 tons for the industry of Britain. There was not one alternative. With this vital information we got on to places like Parsons, and we caused all the electrical industries suddenly to realise that they were going to have to manage without our sort of services. They were big contracting firms who abruptly realised that they were going to be out on a limb. There was a tremendous amount of trouble when everybody, including such people as ICI, began to realise that they were going to be absolutely prevented from getting a good price for their big castings. We'd previously worked for diesel people on hugh crankshafts, and when they considered the sort of argument that we put forward they began to realise what was going on. We said that you couldn't expect in future to make these crankshafts in the United Kingdom, so that all the firms that needed diesel engines, the firms that provided them, would be held to ransom in the Common Market countries: because they could say we will give them a bigger price, and probably our own people will win the order because we'll price them out of the market.

We insisted that there must be at least one place in Britain that is capable of doing this kind of work: our message began to get over. We went to all our MPs. We went to the Trades and Labour councils. We worked a system, which I think probably proved more important than anything else to us at the particular time in question, in which we had a meeting every Saturday morning, to which we invited all the 260 shop stewards. I must admit that normally only about 80 turned up. Incidentally, the same 80 stuck with us to the end. Out of that 80 we selected 8 or 9 who could best represent the decisions of that particular meeting.

We decided that we could not easily involve all of the 27 unions if we were going into negotiations. And so we ended up with about 9 of us: there were about 3 AEU men, an ETU man and rather surprising perhaps, because we were a minority group, there were from the staff a couple of ASTMS chaps, a CAWU man and a DATA man. Certainly it had come as a great shock to many people that staff were so highly involved in all this, but our involvement was essential if we were to put forward an effective viability argument. At the same time, this strategy snookered us a great deal, because we found that once we'd set out to prove our viability we couldn't easily go out on strike. We set out to show to the management that we could prove to them by sheer guts and sheer hard work that we could get back on to a workable footing. But the minute we'd made that statement we were in trouble because we couldn't strike and we had to work hard to try and find other ways to deal with the situation.

We had a first sign of the difficulties we had got into towards the end of August, when the kids were supposed to come and start work after leaving school. The management suddenly knocked off 60 apprentices. We had a hell of a do about that, and we fought and fought. We got involved with the Lord Mayor, (incidentally, a Conservative) because Sir Ron Ironmonger, who was the Labour leader, talked him into thinking about things by saying, 'look, let this be an important feature of your work as Lord Mayor', and in this way got him to work with the Employment Exchange. As a result, although we didn't get any apprentices, what we got was a concession in which we used our apprentice training shop to run training schemes, including a six-week welding scheme and another twelve-week machining scheme for people who had already been in work and left.

This scheme has been set up under the Council and working with British Steel Corporation, and to reach agreement on it we sacrificed a complete overtime ban, which we found was giving us a great number of difficulties because orders started moving out. Of course, we had difficulty with this traditional weapon anyway, because management could say to us, 'until you finish this job we can't give you another one'.

On the broader questions, we found ourselves in a situation in which we were blinded by the UCS example, because when we said work on, everybody said 'well, we can't do it' since everybody knew full well that if we tried to work on in order to establish our case and prove the viability of the plant, the British Steel Corporation would stop the orders. In this way we would probably find that at best we might be able to melt on the first week, forge on the second week, and to start machining on the fourth or fifth week and after that we'd have run ourselves to a standstill. When it came towards the end of September or the beginning of October, management said to us, 'right, we're sorry but we've got to start redundancies due to worsening trade. This, they said was being caused by our overtime ban. We felt we were stuck.

And so we found ourselves confronted by three or four hundred redundancies, which we hammered down by means of a lot of work sharing. We did a great deal of work sharing. At the same time, we also created what we called a 'working arm'. When a person was made redundant we didn't have him in our works, we set him on working for us outside: and we even had the cheek to go and ask for the use of a dining room, one of the works dining rooms, which is now our main office. We asked for it and we were rather surprised that we got it, but as soon as we got it we asked could we have a telephone installed. They've not given us that up to now. Yet we've still got the dining room facility, in which we have people involved in the organising and publicising the work-on and also involved in arranging the work sharing.

We have organised two levies: we have a levy on behalf of the people who are working on and one where people who are involved in the work-sharing come and join those who are working-on. The money that their particular department collects goes as hardship money to that particular area.

I would like to mention two other things. In this struggle we found ourselves in a situation where traditional militancy would have failed. Our plant was looked at very carefully by the British Steel Corporation, who saw our actual viability and studied our viability report, and who saw our reaction to certain other things that were done, which we didn't like particularly, but which helped to save the factory. When they saw that we were not militant but trying to act as responsible workmen they gave us this chance."

This action had clear limits, but it offers a graphic instance of the principle of social auditing, advanced by the Institute for Workers' Control as a necessary part of any strategy of resistance to factory closures.[6]

Footnotes

1. On 21 October "Over 4,500 workers at BSA decided by an overwhelming vote today to conduct a work-in" (*Morning Star*, 22 October 1971). Committees were established among shop stewards to co-ordinate the necessary work (*Financial Times*, 23 October 1971). These called for an immediate public enquiry (*Morning Star*, same date). By the 28th October, stewards had abandoned the "work-in" call, and were urging a strike (*Morning Star, Times, Financial Times*). The following day, the strike meeting attracted "only a handful" (*Times*) and was characterised as "a complete collapse of the union membership at BSA" (*Financial Times*, 29 October 1971).
2. See *Inside Story* No.10, August 1973.

3. Geoffrey Sheriden, interview with Susan Shapiro, *Guardian*, 15 June 1972.
4. It should be noted that full time union officers had been very keenly pushing for action, whilst the workpeople were obviously reluctant to "make matters worse" by pushing the company into liquidation. Many workers were quoted in the press as voicing strong criticism of union leaders.
5. John Gretten *To Sit or Not to Sit? New Society* 15 June 1972, pp.564-6.
6. For a recent treatment, see Coates (editor) *The Right to Useful Work*, Spokesman, Nottingham 1978. Also Barratt Brown: *UCS, the Social Audit*: IWC pamphlet 26, 1971. (Part reproduced below, pp.87 et seq.)

Chapter VI

The Social Audit

The social audit is seen as an attempt to assess, and place before public opinion, some picture of the true socio-economic costs of decisions which are taken within the narrow rationality of enterprise budgets. Any firm may decide on plant closures, even if the plant in question is actually profitable, if still more profitable options present themselves for the exploitation of capital and resources involved. For instance, asset strippers may move in to shut down job opportunities in order to realise property development values. But the result of such actions, which may well be "profit" for small groups of speculators, is often net and unredeemed loss for the community at large. The social costs of turning the Clyde into an even more acutely depressed area than it already was in 1971 included as a minimum the unemployment and social security benefits due to the victims of the process, and very likely also the additional costs of moving, re-employing, housing, educating and providing for an infrastructure of transport and social services for a whole displaced community. Such costs would, of course, fall on the exchequer, or on local rates, and in any event would not affect the internal budget of the old UCS consortium. So the decision to close would ignore them. But ignored or not, these costs would remain very real, and on any calculation they must grossly exceed the cost of maintaining a declining industry over an interim period during which new employment could be devised for an existing community.

WORK-INS, SIT-INS AND INDUSTRIAL DEMOCRACY

At UCS Tony Benn had pressed the Scottish TUC to establish a public enquiry, which, he suggested, should be organised along the following lines:

"A Government statement on UCS is imminent. The indication is that, at best, Fairfields and Linthouse might be saved if private capital could be found and Clydebank closed down. At worst, the whole might founder. Meanwhile, the shop stewards have confirmed their intention of occupying the yards and have received support from the STUC.

Finally, the Industrial Relations Act will soon be in force and could raise doubts as to the legality of sympathy strikes by other dockers, which cannot be ruled out in view of the seriously worsening employment situation.

It is against this background that the trade union movement and the Parliamentary Labour Party have to consider what to do. It is an extremely difficult, important and potentially explosive situation. The proposal that follows is designed to be of real value in clarifying the situation and developing a practical approach to it.

What I am proposing is that the trade union movement should organise a public examination in Clydeback of all the issues raised by UCS bankruptcy, and the government policy to be announced. This public examination would constitute the sort of 'social audit' advocated by the Institute of Workers' Control and would follow the general lines of a Congressional hearing held in public at which those involved would be able to give evidence, submit statements and be asked to amplify what they said. The meeting would be open to the public, including the mass media, but the cross examination of witnesses would be done by the committee and not by TV or newspaper correspondents.

The ideal place to hold it would be in the Clydebank Town Council offices, and under the auspices of the Council.

The composition of the committee would be a matter for decision: it could be a single examiner, or a group of examiners, made up of trade unionists, MPs, and local councillors. Those who would prefer to give evidence might wish to do so as witnesses, rather than as members of the commitee.

In any case the witnessses would need to include all those who had anything to offer to an understanding of the problem and how it might be tackled. These would include the following:

1. The shop stewards
2. District Union officials
3. The provost or town councillors
4. Ken Douglas or other managers

THE SOCIAL AUDIT

5. Mr Hepper or other Board members — especially Mr MacKenzie
6. Professor Ken Alexander
7. The manager of the Employment Exchange
8. Members of the Scottish Economic Planning Council
9. Sir Ian Stewart and perhaps other industrialists
10. Sir William Swallow or other members of the SIB
11. One or all of the 'three wise men'
12. A Government Minister

The form of the public examination would be very simple. The examiners would sit at the table and witnesses would come forward — preferably with a short written statement which they would read into the record, and then would be questioned upon it. If other witnesses wished to submit questions they would be put by examiners.

The examination would go on for as long as was necessary, and afterwards the examiners would confer and announce their preliminary conclusions.

A full transcript, or extensive records of the day's proceedings — together with written submissions would then be published: as a 'White Paper' or 'Red Paper' for all those concerned.

This proposal would of course have to be discussed with and approved by the shop stewards and the trade unions most concerned, before it was made known. It would have to be conducted in deadly earnest against the expected press attacks upon its nature and form.

The object would be to clarify the issues, secure adequate representations of the views of the men concerned, and compel accountability by the Company and the Government to the workers most affected by the decisions taken. This is its real significance, and if it were successful the application of the same principle to other redundancy cases throughout the country might prove possible.

This is the plan in outline, and I suggest that it be cleared with all those involved at once, so that the announcement of the public examination can be made immediately after the Government statement, the date fixed at once and the necessary arrangements made together with the issuing of the invitations."

In the event, the STUC mounted a thorough-going investigation by a team which met for nine days and heard a variety of important evidence on precisely these topics.[1] The IWC submitted various evidence to this enquiry, some of which was subsequently published.[2]

The economic reasoning involved in the proposal for a social audit of the costs of projected plant closures was clearly stated in Michael Barratt Brown's pamphlet, *UCS: The Social Audit*. Now long out of print, this important text put forward the basic arguments which were subsequently developed in the Enquiry organised by the Scottish TUC, and was obviously influential on the Sheffield shop stewards who drafted the River Don alternative plan.

"The crisis of Upper Clyde Shipbuilders", wrote Michael Barratt Brown, "is a microcosm of the crisis of the whole of British Industry in which output has not risen for three years and a growing proportion of men and resources are unemployed. A social audit thus implies: *first*, an examination of the social costs and benefits which have to be taken into account in considering the closing down of two shipbuilding yards on the Clyde, and particularly the implications for employment opportunities; and *secondly* an examination of the political and economic policies of the government within the framework of which the closure is proposed".

Social cost-benefit analysis simply moves the framework of calculations outside the balance-sheet of the individual enterprise, to permit the calculation of the costs and benefits incurred by and bestowed upon the wider society outside its boundaries. If a factory pollutes an adjacent river, this may actually look good within its balance-sheet, because it may thus avoid expensive investment for the safe disposal of its pollutant. But to the water authority struggling to sanitise the river system, to other potential users of the river water, to say nothing of anglers, preservationists and other advocates of conservation, the act of pollution is an act of vandalism which may engender costs (which fall upon a more general public) far greater than the savings (which benefit only the minority of people with an interest in the offending firm). Companies calculate profit and loss with strict attention to the bills they pick up, but with no attention at all to those bills which may be imposed on other people.

But at River Don, the shop stewards themselves

prepared their own defence brief, which made available much of the vital data on the likely repercussions for the British economy of BSC's decision: and this was a model example, not simply of "public relations" as some newspapers described it, but of the fundamental politics of the work-in movement.

Footnotes

1. An interim report of this enquiry was published in the *Trade Union Register 3*, Spokesman 1973.
2. Ken Fleet: *Whatever Happened at UCS?* IWC Pamphlet 28; Robin Murray: *The Anatomy of Bankruptcy*, Spokesman 1972.

Appendix: The Social Audit

Michael Barratt Brown's extended review of the economic effects of the closure of UCS was the first full-scale attempt to show what a social audit should try to do, within the framework proposed by the Institute for Workers' Control. Part of his text is reproduced here, as an example of the kinds of argument involved in the process.

It is essential first in considering social costs and benefits to remember the old adage of the economist, that 'bygones are bygones'. This does not mean that one should fail to learn lessons from the past; it means that in considering new investment today, yesterday's investments are largely irrelevant. It makes no more sense and no less sense to talk about throwing good money after bad than it does to talk about throwing away assets that have had great value in the past. This is of particular importance in the case of UCS because the fact has to be faced that large sums of money have in the past been provided for the company mainly from Government sources.

Table 1

Capital Structure and History of UCS

Nov. 1965	Government loan to Fairfields of £1m.
Dec. 1965	Fairfield established with Share Capital of £2m of which Government provided 50%, Trade Unions 10% and private investors 40%. Government advances £1m.

WORK-INS, SIT-INS AND INDUSTRIAL DEMOCRACY

Jan. 1968	UCS formed with Share Capital plus Rights offer of which Fairfields 35%, John Brown 30%, Yarrow 20%, Alexander Stephens 10% and Charles Connell 5%.	£4m £1m
Mar. 1969	Shipbuilding Industry Board (SIB) loan	£3m
June 1969	Government Loans and Grants	£9.3m
Dec. 1969	SIB Second Loan	£7m
Feb. 1971	Yarrow hived off from UCS and given a Government Loan of £4.5m.	
June 1971	Government refuses loan to UCS of £6m.	

Source: *Labour Research,* August 1971.

It will be seen that Government funds to the extent of some £21m have been made available, almost all as loans to Fairfields and UCS. This sum must be seen in context. It should be set against the total of £57.5m of loans and grants which the Shipbuilding Industry Board was empowered under the 1967 Act to make available. £25m was provided over the same period to Harland and Wolff, of Belfast, and a further £7m provided in July of this year, together with a 47% Stormont Government holding in the equity. In 1965 Harland and Wolff claimed an annual production capacity of 200,000 grt compared with UCS capacity (excluding Yarrow and the now closed Alexander Stepehens Yard) of about 250,000 grt. For a further financial comparison it might be added that the UCS order book in June of 1971 stood at around £90 millions.

What has been invested in the past is no necessary test of what should be done in the future. UCS inherited losses of £4.2m from John Brown's. This was not regarded by the Geddes Committee as an argument against the formation of UCS, although it was regarded by the Labour Government as a reason for making changes in the senior management. We shall return to this point later.

The crucial question is what should be done with the resources we have at our disposal today; and this is as true for society as a whole as it is for a single firm. Resources which we decide to invest today in one project are not available for others. Even if there are unemployment resources of men and machinery, while this gives an added reason for making an early decision, to prevent further waste, it does not alter the fact that a decision to invest resources (of materials and land as well as of skilled workers and managers) in one place means that they cannot be invested somewhere else. The more unemployed resources there are, of course, the larger the social benefits in relation to social costs of setting them to work. What must be borne in mind is that it still matters what those resources are set to work on.

It is not difficult to examine the accounts of a company and to determine from them where profits and losses have been made, where unit costs have risen or sales have fallen for example. This

THE SOCIAL AUDIT

does not give a sure guide for investment in the future, because past experience is not likely to be repeated exactly. Together with other information about the future that is available past experience does however, give the management of a company some guide for its investment decisions. The expected return to capital over a period of years from different projects can be estimated and the most profitable projects selected. But how are we to examine the social amounts, where we are concerned with social costs and benefits and not the private profits and loss accounts of companies? On what criteria should governments decide where to invest resources in the interests of society as a whole? Past experience of evident social costs and benefits will be useful and estimates can be made as for a private company of the return to capital invested in certain schemes, as in the nationalised industries where goods or services are sold to the public. Such estimates could be made about investment in shipbuilding and these were presumably made by the Advisory Group on Shipbuilding on the Upper Clyde, in deciding that only the Govan/Linthouse site formed a basis for an investment "with good prospects of profitability".

What then are the considerations that a social audit must take into account over and above the expectations of return to capital? There are all the external economies and diseconomies, in the economists jargon: that is those external to the individual company. But in addition there is the benefit of the full employment of resources and its obverse, the costs of unemployment; and there are other benefits which we may bunch together under the general heading of welfare. How can all these be quantified so as to compare one scheme with another? Let us consider them one by one.

a. *External Economies.* These arise mainly from the planning of investment: e.g., in developing a multi-purpose port with ore and oil terminals, storage and refining or processing facilities, so that the various projects are mutually beneficial. No individual company would necessarily have known what the others were going to do; so that none might have found these projects profitable on their own. In relation to UCS, a joint project involving the British Steel Corporation, which not only supplies the steel to UCS from its Cambuslang works but is also a major operator of ore carriers, was put forward by John Hughes in an earlier pamphlet issued by the Institute for Workers' Control.* Such joint projects could be and should be costed on as alternatives to an individual company estimate.

b. *External Costs.* Examples of these are pollution of land, air and water, destruction or wastage of natural assets, congestion and danger to life and limb on the road, and in the towns and cities. These may appear at first sight to be hard to quantify, but some

UCS. Institute for Workers' Control Pamphlet No.25.

estimate can be made of the costs of paintwork, repair of buildings, cleaning away rubbish, clearing rivers, loss of renewable materials, time lost by delay, and hospital costs, from accidents.

In this respect UCS cannot be considered except in relation to the whole Clyde Estuary Development. There have been far too much secrecy and too little discussion of the Metra-Weddle Report, the reports of the Inspector of Nuclear Installations, not to mention the two nuclear submarine bases.

c. *Full Employment.* By far the most important resource at our disposal is the human resource — the skills and energy of human labour — and the next section will be devoted to this subject. There are however other resources of machinery and plant and of social infrastructure — houses, road, railways, water supply, drains, schools and so on. The closing down of a major centre of employment as at Clydebank that led to a whole area being abandoned and the people moving elsewhere would involve a great wastage of existing social equipment. New houses, schools, roads, drains etc., would have to be built in the places to which the people had to move. Such costs are social costs, of course, and do not enter into the books of the company which decides to move its plant from Scotland to the outskirts of London. But they can easily be quantified on two assumptions: of 5,000 workers and their families, and of 15,000, having to be resettled.

Table 2

Unit Cost of Public Capital Expenditure 1968

Item	*Unit Cost* £	*Cost per 5,000* £m	*Cost per 15,000* £m
Housing			
Erection	3,000	15	45
Site works	700	3.5	10.5
Land	450	2.25	6.75
Total	4,150	20.75	62.25
Schools			
Primary	250	1.25	3.75
Secondary	450	2.25	6.75
Roads			
Per mile	500,000	5.0	10.0
Hospitals			
Per bed	15,000	3.0	6.0
Total	6,500	32.25	96.75

Note. It is assumed that each family needs one house, one place at primary and one at secondary school at any time, and that one mile of new road is required per 1,000 people and one hospital bed for twenty-five families.
Source: HM Treasury *Unit Costs of Public Expenditure.*

THE SOCIAL AUDIT

The implications of the figures in Table 2 are remarkable. The cost of resettling 5,000 families in areas where accommodation and social facilities are already fully used, so that new construction would be required amounts to the considerable figure of over £32m, or roughly £6,500 per family. It might be added that since 1968 all prices have risen by about 25%, so that the figures could now be around £8,000 per family, or £40m for 5,000 families.

d. *Welfare.* Under this heading may be included many costs like those of education, health and other social services which can be quantified in terms of increased quantity of output, less time lost from illness and accidents, and the maintenance of demand at a minimum level in periods of unemployment. Much less easily quantifiable are the benefits derived from parks and trees and pleasant surroundings, and neighbours including relatives and close friends. A price can of course be put upon this by asking people how much more pay they would need in a new job in order to attract them to move away from home. There is also the age-old problem of the economist and political scientist, of how to compare one man's welfare and another's or one man's gain in welfare with another's loss of welfare. One principle which has been widely accepted is particularly relevant to Clydeside, where unemployment is already high and poverty widespread. This is that since we satisfy our most urgent wants first, the richer we are the less urgent are the wants we satisfy. Thus, in the famous phrase of A.C. Pigou: "Any cause which increases the absolute share of real income in the hands of the poor, provided that it does not lead to a contraction in the size of the national income from any point of view, will in general increase economic welfare".* A second principle is becoming equally widely accepted, that is that the principle of 'no taxation without representation', which provided the justification for establishing the power of Parliament over Government, must be extended to involve people at every level of society — in enterprise and localities — in the decisions that most closely affect them.

It has already been suggested that labour is the most important resource that we have at our disposal and that there may be quite large costs in moving labour to jobs rather than bringing jobs to the workers. John Hughes in an earlier pamphlet of the Institute for Workers' Control gave figures for unemployment in Scotland and Great Britain respectively which may be amplified and set out as in Table 3.

---

*A.C. Pigou, *Economics of Welfare*, p.89.

Table 3
Employment and Unemployment in Great Britain and Scotland (Male and Female)

Year and Month	Employment (000's)		Unemployment (000's)		Rate %	
	G.B.	Scotland	G.B.	Scotland	G.B.	Scotland
1965 June	23,147	2,139	308	62.2	1.3	2.8
1966 ..	23,301	2,143	323	58.8	1.4	2.7
1967 ..	22,828	2,100	512	79.5	2.2	3.7
1968 ..	22,645	2,086	541	79.6	2.3	3.7
1969 ..	22,600	2,091	535	78.2	2.3	3.6
1970 ..	22,404	2,077	573	89.4	2.5	4.1
1971 Dec.	22,328	2.071	589	98.0	2.6	4.5
1971 June	—	—	740	118.9	3.2	5.5
1965-71	—819	—68	+432	+56.7	—	—

Source: *DEP Gazette* July 1971.

The figures in Table 3 certainly shows that the average rate of unemployment in Scotland has tended to be well above that of Great Britain as a whole but they also reveal that it has risen ahead of that in Britain. If we take male unemployment only, since most of the shipyard workers are men, we may notice an even more serious gap between numbers of unemployed and numbers of vacancies for employment notified to the Labour exchanges.

Table 4
Men Unemployed and Job Vacancies Great Britain and Scotland 1966-71

	Unemployed per ten vacancies	
Year	Great Britain	Scotland
1966	14	47
1970	47	114
1971	85	246

What is most serious for the Clydeside workers, unemployment is worst on the Clydeside and in the Glasgow area than elsewhere in Scotland. The rates of unemployment for men and women in mid-1971 were 5.5% for Scotland as a whole and 5.8% for Scottish Development Areas, but 6.5% in Glasgow, 7.4% in Dumbarton, 8.1% in Greenock and 14.3% in Bathgate. The figures are that much worse for men, because women tend not to register when they know work is unavailable. To complete the picture we may add that opportunities for female employment are no better than in the rest of the country. About a half of the women aged 16-64 have full time or part-time work which is only slightly less than the average for Britain as a whole.

THE SOCIAL AUDIT

How far can the cost of unemployment be quantified? First, a simple calculation can be made of the cost of such unemployment as we have been discussing, in terms of dole and supplementary benefit. Frank Field in a recent article in *Tribune* (June 6) did the arithmetic for the prospective loss of jobs on Clydeside taking into account average supplementary benefit payments in Scotland. The figures are summarised in Table 5, based on two alternative assumptions: of unemployment being limited to the 5,000 immediately laid off and of it involving through subcontractors and other multiplier effects up to 27,000 as the Scottish TUC has suggested. Frank Field further assumed that on the most hopeful estimates based on current trends, 70% of these will be out of work for an average six months, another 13% for a year and the remainder of an average of three years.

Table 5
Social Security Cost of Unemployment

Costs	Rate per week per family (£)	Assuming 5,000 Unemployed (£m)	Assuming 27,000 Unemployed (£m)
a. 70% unemployed for 6 months			
35% men without working wives			
Supplementary Benefit (avg.)*	13.60	0.62	3.35
— 35% with working wives			
Flat rate (avg.)	5.00	0.39	2.10
Wage related (avg.)	3.50		
b. 13% unemployed for 1 year			
— 6.5% without working wives	13.60	0.22	1.19
— 6.5% with working wives			
6 months @	8.50	0.07	0.38
6 months @	5.00	0.04	0.21
c. 17% unemployed for 3 years			
— 8.5% without working wives	13.60	0.9	4.85
— 8.5% with working wives			
6 months @	8.50	0.56	3.00
2½ years @	5.00	0.34	1.85
d. Total	10.68	3.14	16.93

*after deducting 90p family allowance and assuming two children per family.

Next one may note that redundancy payments would at least double these figures, so that costs to Government revenue of the order of £15m might be involved. This calculation serves to set in proper perspective the sums of money involved. UCS asked the Government for a further loan of £6m. It does not, of course, prove that this investment should have been made in UCS. The claims of UCS to Government finance will have to be examined in their own right. We shall proceed to do this in a moment. What we have discovered so far is a basis for determining the additional cost of employing a man on Clydeside compared with leaving him unemployed. If average wages in shipbuilding in Scotland are shall we say £25.00 per week and men are prepared to work as labourers at, shall we say, £16.00 per week, then the difference between these figures and the £10.68 which was found to be the average weekly cost of dole and supplementary benefit, can be regarded as the social cost of employing an unemployed man on Clydeside. For there to be a social benefit arising from his work his weekly labour would have to add a value in excess of this. Of course, this principle could not be universally applied to the whole national labour force or there would be no taxable incomes from which transfers to the unemployed could be made. But this does not prevent the application where some 5% of resources are unemployed. For ensuring full employment it should not be difficult to find schemes which fulfilled this necessary requirement, although we should still want to find schemes in which the value added by the labour of each newly employed man was as high as it could be.

It is now necessary to consider the general framework of Government economic policies within which unemployment on Clydeside is conceived. For, even if we exclude the possibility of a Tory Government being prejudiced against a company which had been reconstructed with Government and even Trade Union capital, there remains the possibility that unemployment is itself being used as an instrument of policy.

There are several reasons why this is done; and these several reasons, together, make up a coherent economic policy, however misguided it may appear to be.

a. There is first the argument that full employment at home tends to pull in additional imports with increased home consumption which cannot be paid for by additional exports. A measure of unemployment is therefore required, so it is argued, in order to reduce imports and encourage firms to look to the export market rather than to the home market for their growth. Quite apart from the fact that the result of this policy, pursued by successive government, has, in every case, been a generally deflated level of economic activity in which investment is deferred and costs rise so that exporting becomes more, not less, difficult, there is a special reason why the policy is inappropriate for the Shipbuilding Industry. Unfortunately, governments have not usually discriminated in their measures of deflation between one industry and another; and the fact is that the shipbuilding industry exports a particularly high proportion of its output (40% to 50% of merchant ships; 25% of all ships including naval vessels*), and, what is more, only a very small proportion of its input (less than a tenth compared with about a fifth for all industry), consists of imports. Of course shipyard workers like other workers, buy foreign goods and may take holidays abroad when the money is good; but a cut-back to their industry has evidently a specially adverse balance of payments effect.

This becomes very clear if we consider the vlaue of UK imports and exports of ships in the last few years and consider also the trade in shipping services, as set out in Table 6.

Table 6.

UK Imports and Exports of Ships and Shipping Services

Year	Ships (£m)			Shipping Services (£m)		
	Imports	Exports	Balance	Imports	Exports	Balance
1964	19	30	+11	724	687	—7
1965	26	34	+ 8	728	725	—3
1966	9	48	+38	716	718	+2
1967	22	69	+47	780	798	+18
1968	34	82	+48	895	956	+61
1969	39	62	+23	914	959	+44
1970	31.5	61	+30	1,087	1,073	—14

Source: *Overseas Trade Accounts of the UK.*

Although there has been a positive balance of trade in ships, it cannot be a matter for satisfaction that, although about half of all shipping built in the UK is exported, nevertheless so much as a third of all shipping ordered by shipping lines comes from abroad. What is more the balance on shipping services shows that UK shipping lines are only carrying about a half of the goods leaving and entering this country.

b. An additional argument concerned with the UK balance of payments has recently been adduced by Government spokesmen. Not only was a large surplus on UK payments required to meet the immediate adverse effects on our trade from entry into Europe, but the long-run competitive position of British industry in the Common Market required what is euphemistically described as a "slimming" process throughout industry. It is evidently the workers who are destined for slimming since the intention behind the phrase is that firms could cut down on their labour force, so as to reduce their labour costs in order to be able to compete with West European

*Source: *Annual Abstract of Statistics*, Table 200.

firms on equal terms. Where necessary this may involve the closure of whole plants, the bankruptcy of whole companies. This might as well be faced now, it is argued, since it will certainly have to be faced when we enter the Common Market and British industry loses the protection of tariffs and other devices which at present serve to keep out the cheaper foreign product.

Now, apart from the fact that this might be a good reason for not entering such a competitive struggle, it is important to grasp the logical implications of the argument. In theory, under the Rome Treaty (Article 92), no member state of the European Economic Community may subsidise production in its own industries in a way which discriminates against those of other member states. Of course in fact there are many loopholes and the rules of fair and free competition enshrined in the Treaty are not yet fully enforced. Nevertheless, the objective which is wholeheartedly endorsed by the Conservative Government is that competition should be unrestrained. The implication of this must be duly recognised. Since in economic struggles the rule is that "winner takes all and the devil take the hindmost", the British people could quite quickly find themselves with a small number of individually quite large competitive firms (the ones, perhaps, whose chairmen advertise in the *Times* their support for the Common Market) still in business and the rest bankrupt and their workers redundant. Whether any ship-building firm survived this sudden exposure to the full blast of foreign competition would depend on Government orders e.g. for naval vessels as at Yarrow and Vickers. We shall consider in a moment what might be the real competitive strength of British Shipbuilding in general, and UCS in particular, with the same degree of protection that other ship-building yards in the EEC at present get away with. The general principle of encouraging competition in industry needs first to be carefully examined.

c. What Mr John Davies, the Conservative Minister of Trade and Industry, has described with enthusiasm as the "abrasive effects of competition", and the faith that we have just seen that the Conservatives place in "slimming", add up to a view of economic activity that is indeed very close to that of Adam Smith and the "invisible hand" which equates private greed and public benefit. For the shipyard workers of the Upper Clyde all this means that if their firm goes bust that is all to the good because they will then be free to move to other firms in other industries in other parts of Britain, indeed in other parts of Europe perhaps, which are proving themselves more efficient in the competitive struggle. Now such a statement will no doubt be greeted with horse laughter at Clydebank. With the rate of unemployment in Glasgow at 6.5% (10% for men) and in Britain as a whole of 3.2% (4.5% for men) the phrases in the Report of the Advisory Group on Shipbuilding on the Upper Clyde about Government and local authority assistance in the "redeployment" of the 5,000 redundant staff and workers from UCS must appear to be just pie in the sky. These advisors and the Government that appointed them may, however, genuinely believe that we are still living in a nineteenth century world of small competitive companies all at roughly similar levels of technology — some more successful than others — and that the more successful will have vacancies to take up those workers who find themselves in less successful companies. It would be a pretty picture if it ever existed.

The facts are otherwise. In the first place, the vacancies notified to Employment Exchanges today number some 200,000 (74,000 for adult males) and the wholly unemployed number 700,000 (600,000 of them for males). In Scotland the relative figures we saw to be still more ill-balanced. In the second place, and this is the crucial point in our economy today, the sources of finance for investment are increasingly concentrated in a few large companies. About 100 companies take up over 90% of all new funds issued on the London Stock Exchange and generate from their own sources about 40% of all such internal funds for investment among companies quoted on the Stock Exchange.[1] Yet in these quoted companies, they employ less than a fifth of all the workers. The giant company with the capital to invest is operating at very high levels of technology driven by the competitive economic struggle to seek out monopolistic positions at the very frontiers of technology. With the most advanced automated production they provide the growth points of production but they are not interested in taking on extra workers. This is why the proportion of funds to provide employment has to come increasingly from the Government. Whether those funds should be invested in shipbuilding we shall consider in a moment. There remains to be examined one further reason for Government policies designed to create unemployment.

d. This is the possibility that unemployment is being deliberately created in order to reduce the pressures of Trade Unions for wage increases. One of the "disciplines of the market" which the Conservative leaders are forever invoking is the discipline of the *labour* market. In down to earth terms this means quite frankly the queue at the factory gate. Now it is a fact that in the last decade both the shares of profit in the UK. National income and post-tax rates of profit of UK companies have been falling.[2] The fall has been particularly steep since 1964. It is also a fact that profits tend to fall in periods of slump or stagnation and the rate of growth in real terms of the UK national product in the six years 1964-70 (averaging 2.2% p.a.) has been little more than a half of that achieved in the previous seven years 1958-64. (3.7% p.a.) Moreover, it is not expected that there will be any growth at all in 1971. This has been the price of the defence of the balance of payments at all costs.[3] But whereas other periods of slump and stagnation since 1945 have been short-lived, this most recent period has lasted for more than three years (the national income (GDP) index based on 1963 = 100, reached 116 in mid-1968; it was standing at 116 in mid-1971). Moreover, in previous periods of history a slump of this duration would have been accompanied by falling wages as unemployment rose. This time the Trade Unions have gone far to maintain real wages for their members. This has been despite the very sharply rising prices as employers have sought to pass on their rising unit costs (compounded of higher money wages and lower capacity working) in higher prices to the public.*

The results of such a rise in prices as has occurred in the last year (10% in one year) is, however, to threaten the whole post-devaluation competitive position of British industry in world markets; and the Conservative Government, not daring to increase industry's capacity working by stimulating the home market (apart from the mini measures of Mr Barber's mini budget in July) for fear of pulling in imports in excess of exports just before our entry to the Common Market, has perhaps decided to bring down wages and prices by sharply increasing unemployment. This was the old-fashioned, pre-Keynesian remedy for re-establishing rates of profit. We are hearing once more the cry that industry must have the profits to invest in new plant and to create new opportunities for employment. What Keynes taught, but evidently to little effect, was that businessmen invest, not when their past profits have created savings for investment, but when the expectation of an expanding market for their products leads them to believe in a profitable return from investment. Certainly this must be the conclusion from the absolute failure of investment in manufacturing industry to rise over the last three years and from the sharp decline of forward looking indicators of such investment in the last months when unemployment has been rising and the Conservative Government claims that price increases are under control. For the simple dilemma, which Marx explained a hundred years ago, still faces every capitalist; he must cut his wage costs or raise his prices to make profits if he is to stay in the competitive economic struggle; but if all capitalists do likewise who is to buy the goods the capital is set to produce? And once unemployment and reduced incomes emerge in one industry or area, a whole vicious downward cycle of declining incomes and economic activity may be generated. We have only avoided such deep recessions of activity since the war by means of massive Government expenditures. Have the Conservative Government really decided in their enthusiasm to

---

*The mechanism of the process is fully explained in the evidence of the Institute for Workers' Control submitted to the Wilberforce Court of Enquiry into pay into Electricity Workers and published as Pamphlet No.24, *Trade Unions and Rising Prices*.

cut the rate of income tax that this whole post-war era of full employment is to be ended? It certainly seems so; and the case of UCS may be taken as a test of whether they can get away with it.

Footnotes

1. For details see M. Barratt Brown *Who Controls Industry?* in K. Coates (ed) *Can the Workers Run Industry?*
2. The detailed facts and figures are to be found in A. Glyn and R. Sutcliffe "The Collapse of UK Profits" *New Left Review* No.66 March-April 1971.
3. For details see M. Barratt Brown "Two halves of a Decade" *Trade Union Register 1970*, p.307.

Chapter VII

Spreading out all over . . .

All the events so far described began within six months of one another. UCS was occupied at the end of July 1971. The sit-in at Plessey's in Dumbartonshire began on 3rd September. During the same month, the work-on at River Don was the first major extension of workplace occupations from Scotland to England. A couple of days after the announcement of the Sheffield Steelworkers' initiative, an engineering establishment in the same city, Snow Engineering, was occupied. A nine-day sit-in against redundancy ended when the workers found themselves locked out, because they had begun to return home in the evenings to sleep. It was at the end of October that the various plans for action at BSA in Birmingham collapsed. Next month there was a short sit-in in Manchester, and after a Christmas lull, at the opening of the New Year, both Allis Chalmers in Mold and Fisher-Bendix at Kirkby were taken over by their workpeople.

All except one of these stay-ins were directed against redundancy. More protests of the same kind were to erupt throughout 1972.

The Sit-in as an all-purpose strike sanction

By March 1972 the successes in opposing redundancy by occupation had become so evident as to encourage a significant extension of the sit-in, in the course of a novel campaign of actions supporting conventional pay claims in the engineering industry in Lancashire. There had already been a brief but exemplary action by Cooperative Insurance employees in Manchester in November 1971. 1,800 members of the ASTMS sat in for less than 24 hours in pursuit of a pay claim, with evident success. Later, in February the following year, there was a similar, longer action at Leicester Photographic and Litho Services. When the Engineering Employers' federation rejected the national wage demands of the Confederation of Shipbuilding and Engineering Unions, the unions decided to press the same claims plant by plant, and in the Manchester region this produced a wave of strikes, quickly followed by a large number of sit-ins.[1] On the 15th March the Guest, Keen and Nettlefold's works at Bredbury, near Stockport, was occupied by its 900 workers, who sat in for 69 days. Within two months, more than thirty Lancashire factories had been taken over by their workers, and by the end of June some fifty settlements had been reached, half of them as a result of sit-ins, while a number of sit-ins were still going on. It was estimated that between 25,000 and 30,00 workers in the Greater Manchester area were involved in these occupations. There was some fallout from this campaign in Yorkshire, where plants were taken over in Leeds and Sheffield, and in the Greater London Area. At Stanmore Engineering, of Middlesex, the predominantly immigrant labour force was evicted and locked out. With one small exception, no one else involved in this upsurge shared this fate. Some firms tried to incommode their rebellious employees by depriving them of power for heating and lighting, although often this response failed to bite when workers took over the keys to the appropriate switch-rooms. The only other effective reprisal by an employer involved a civil action for trespass, taken by a small entrepreneur in Manchester against her 22 employees. She was enabled to proceed in this way because it soon became apparent that she intended to get out of business altogether, and consequently was uninhibited about the effects of her action.

SPREADING OUT ALL OVER . . .

The total picture of the Lancashire movement was assessed in the periodical *New Society*[2] as follows:

South Lancashire Engineers' Sit-Ins

Firm	Started	Duration in days	No. manual workers Involved	Comments
James Mills	15.3.72	69	900	Part of GKN steel grp.
Laurence Scott	23.3.72	37	500	Electric Motors
Davies & Metcalfe	23.3.72	27	150	Stockport
Mirrlees Blackstone	27.3.72	61	950	
E. Peart	27.3.72	40	110	Gas Engineers in Hyde
BSC, Openshaw	28.3.72	56	360	
BSC, Trafford Park	28.3.72	53	280	
Serck Heat Transfer	28.3.72	51	110	
BSC, Warrington	29.3.72	55	176	
Ruston Paxman	29.3.72	*	1,000	Part of GEC
Flexibox, Sharston	30.3.72	57	80	Part of Burmah Oil grp.
GEC Switchgear	30.3.72	65	600	Openshaw
Conveyancer Trucks	30.3.72	9	480	
Archibald Edmeston	4.4.72	46	100	Eccles
Follows & Bate	4.4.72	3	240	Makers of lawn mowers
Francis Shaw	5.4.72	38	450	Two sister companies
Joseph Robinson	5.4.72	52	50	
Hawker Siddeley Aviation	5.4.72	*	1,250	Woodford

continued on page 104

continued from page 103

Metal Box Altrincham	7.4.72	*	250
Linotype, Altrincham	7.4.72	43	500 An American controlled printers
Simon-Vicars	7.4.72	15	280 Warrington
Viking	12.4.72	*	100 Stockport
Frederick Smith	13.4.72	23	850 Part of GEC
Record Electrical	13.4.72	42	280
Kearns Richards	14.4.72	36	270 Part of the Stavely grp.
Mathew Swain	18.4.72	4	130
Capper Neill	20.4.72	16	85 Warrington
Wingrove & Rogers	25.4.72	*	96 At Liverpool, next to Fisher-Bendix
Bason & Son	28.4.72	*	47
Ferranti Hollinwood	11.5.72	22	2,300 All these Ferranti plants
Ferranti Cairo Mill	11.5.72	22	670 are round Oldham: the
Ferranti Gem Mill	16.5.72	17	650 one at Wythenshawe, the
Ferranti Barry Street	16.5.72	18	450 other side of Manchester,
Ferranti Moston	23.5.72	11	900 escaped without a sit-in

*Not available.

NB: This list is as full as possible, but there may be other cases, given the difficulty of tracing statistics. No. of workers involved is approximate.

While occupations as forms of resistance to redundancy received, in general, dispassionate if not actually sympathetic coverage in the responsible press, the extension of the movement to cover pay claims was taken very much amiss by the national newspapers.

At the end of the Lancashire disputes, an EEF spokesman claimed that the employers had "given the unions a mauling".[3] But the union organiser, John Tocher, insisted that the campaign was primarily responsible for the resumption of negotiations, which otherwise would not have taken place. Once these negotiations were under way, there was general speculation about whether the sit-in movement had passed its peak. But not only did sit-ins against redundancy continue. So did sit-ins in pursuit of wage claims one observer counted 38 between June 1972 and the end of 1975.

Other actions during 1972

Immediately after the Lancashire movement, new initiatives quickly appeared: at the Glasgow firm of Charles MacNeill; at Thornycroft, a subsidiary of the British Leyland combine; at CAV Fazakerly; at BP Chemicals, Stroud, in Gloucestershire; and at Gainsborough-Cornard's, a company in Great Yarmouth owned by Viyella. There was also an extended sit-in by staff at the AUEW head office.

The Thorneycroft workers took over their plant in mid-August, with a view to preventing the dismissal of the whole workforce, the sale of the company to an American firm, and the sale of the land and factory-buildings to a property developer. They made sure that never less than 20 per cent of the labour force remained in occupation of the plant at any one time, and after a three month seige, which provoked two one-day solidarity stoppages from the whole British Leyland combine, agreement was reached that 738 of the original 1,100 employees would remain on the books of the new company taking over the plant, that no one would be compulsorily dismissed, and that there would be a six-month breathing-space in which workers who were not required by the Eaton Corporation (the firm in question) would be found alternative jobs. To underpin this arrangement, British Leyland agreed to provide orders for a minimum of three years.

At CAV, a diesel pump manufactory in the Liverpool region, (Fazakerly) it was learnt in late September 1972 that the work of the firm was to be transferred to one of the Lucas Combine's London plants. Clerical workers were among those who joined the resultant sit-in, which also took control of a boiler-house serving another Lucas plant next door. In all 1,200 employees were involved, and their occupation was supported from the beginning by a levy on the 500 workers in the neighbouring Lucas factory. All-Merseyside conferences of shop-stewards were convened to support the Fazakerly workers, who were still receiving active support months after their action started, in September 1972.

Also in that same September, 500 employees of BP Chemicals took over the Stroud plant in order to stop the sale of a casein processing department, employing 100 people. Previously the same year, a package-manufacturing department had been hived-off, with a loss of 200 jobs. Workers feared further redundancies in an area with few alternative employment prospects. By 19th October, the employers conceded defeat, and all the threatened jobs were safeguarded. The Great Yarmouth textile workers, at the Carrington-Viyella subsidiary, were less fortunate: 300 of them began occupation in early September, to prevent an announced shutdown. The final agreement involved higher severance pay.

Besides these actions, each of which, before the advent of the UCS occupation, would have been considered most spectacular events, the last half of 1972 saw many more modest occupations, directed against victimisation (at Milford Haven, in the Foster-Wheeler plant; and at the Brotherhood works at Peterborough); or against unsuitable holiday arrangements (at the Swindon plant of Garrard Engineering); or to impose negotiations on redundancy or severance arrangements, or simply in pursuit of claims on wages, hours or conditions of work. Plessey's were to experience more sit-ins, at Upminster and Nottingham; Tube Investments were hit, at Walsall; as were Pirelli's at Aberdare and a number of other combines.

Each time a major combine was affected even at its most peripheral outposts, the idea of factory occupation received further legitimation, since the first response of any workers involved in such circumstances was to approach their fellow-employees in the company's other plants for aid and support. If Jim Airlie's proposals for all out action by combine committees did not normally receive much sympathy, this was partly because these committees were generally much weaker than other sections of the trade union movement, and partly because of predictable difficulties in co-ordinating action between widely divergent sectors, scattered often over great distances. Yet solidarity actions on a lower level of response than strikes were very common indeed: transfers of production were often blacked, and supporting levies, meetings and similar kinds of moral encouragement all had a two-way effect, helping those who had decided to sit-in, and at the same time rendering the sit-in thinkable to a wider constituency.

The Briant Work-in

In the summer of 1972 there was another spectacular work-in. On 21st June the management of Briant Colour Printing announced that the firm was about to go into liquidation. Briant's, conveniently placed in London's Old Kent Road, employed some 200 workpeople.

This was to be the first large-scale long-term occupation in the printing industry, although McCormick Screen Printing in Glasgow had a short work-in in

November 1971, and Briant's workers themselves had in April 1971, before the outbreak at UCS, successfully opposed 60 redundancies by sitting-in. The action had lasted for one day. (There had also been, as we have seen, during February 1972, a sit-in in Leicester by 28 members of SLADE in pursuit of a pay-claim.)

The Briant work-in provided a real breakthrough in communications since the workers could publish their own propaganda. Even though D.G. Syder, the owner, had installed the most modern equipment, he and his creditors were determined to liquidate: yet from the first moment of the occupation pressure from the unions guaranteed continuous supplies of paper and ink to the work-in. It published a newspaper for the UCS stewards, thousands of posters for the dockers during the National Industrial Relations Court actions against the blacking of container firms, and a whole volume of other trade union work. When Government inspectors called to ensure that appropriate purchase tax was levied on the products of the occupation, they were chided by the workers, who accused them of associating the Government with an act of rebellion. But during the civil service dispute on salaries, the same tax inspectors brought in a contract for their own strike pamphlets, which were then printed on the Briant presses.

Levies on the printing unions, and considerable support from other trade unionists in London, from the Kent Miners, and from many other groups of organised workers, enabled the work-in to take financial responsibility for electricity and phone bills, when the threat was made to disconnect the factory. Various attempts at legal intimidation were made by the owner, but writs were either ignored or publicly burnt, and each new intervention in the Courts brought large public demonstrations of trade unionists to the support of the printworkers.[4] At the end of the action there were still 110 workers in occupation, and after it became quite clear that the workpeople would not in any circumstances hand over the company's books to the liquidator, legal actions were ceased and Briant's was sold for a sum of about £300,000 to another company which undertook to continue production.

This in turn, later pulled out, but its closure did not provoke a repetition of the occupation by the workers. Be that as it may, every precaution was taken to prevent a second work-in. The workers arrived on a Monday morning having been sent their notices over the weekend, to find the factory under strong guard by a Security Company and numerous fierce-looking alsation dogs. The new company's ruthless tactics certainly contributed to its success in closing the enterprise down, but very possibly the unions were also suffering from battle-fatigue.

The extent of the movement

In September 1972 the Metra Consulting Group produced a first survey of some of the sit-ins which had already taken place, omitting UCS, partly because it had already been extensively reported.[5] They compiled the following estimates of their frequency and seriousness during the first six months of 1972.

	Jan.	Feb.	March	1972 April	May	June
No. of workers involved in sit-ins starting in	1,000	—	5,800	6,100	7,800	4,200
No. of workers involved in sit-ins in progress	1,100	800	5,800	11,800	17,300	13,900
No. of work days "lost"	—	—	25,000	17,300	219,000	n.a.

This last measure can only apply to occupations in pursuit of claims other than those concerning dismissal, so work-ins and sit-ins against redundancy are obviously excluded from the tally. Indeed, to be just, they should often be styled "working-days gained", a fact which has no doubt discouraged other statisticians from undue curiosity in the matter.

An alternative source estimates that, by the end of 1972, "more than 69,000 workers had taken part in occupations; 16,000 in 1971 and 53,000 in 1972". All such figures, however, are rather precariously established. First, there is no official machinery for reporting sit-ins or work-ins apart from the generality of strikes, with which they may be quite inappropriately bracketed. Secondly, as the phenomenon of factory occupation became more common, so it became less newsworthy, and the press covered it more and more episodically. Thirdly, occupations may be partial in two different senses: they may involve only one part of a wider establishment, or a smaller group of workpeople than the full labour force may occupy a whole establishment. It is often difficult to determine, from press reports, what has been the precise extent of worker involvement in such actions. It may be objected that, when counting the number of workers on strike, no one is preoccupied with the distinction between active and passive supporters of the event: but where sit-ins are opposing dismissals, this objection does not have quite the same force as it would in the case of a more conventional dispute, because after dismissal some people will seek alternative work, some older workers will in fact retire, and only a proportion may regard themselves as part of any continuing oppositional movement. As we have already seen in the early case of Plessey Alexandria, 250 dismissals took place on 3rd September 1971; 150-200 "regulars" were claimed as assisting the occupation in mid-October; 70 people survived to take up jobs with the new Lyon-Plessey consortium at the end of the action. The same erosion was a factor in very many similar actions. It poses some difficulty for statisticians. The problem is that we have no reason to suppose any very consistent pattern in this kind of decline, because it will vary not only with the internal composition of the dismissed workforce (its age-structure, the proportion of male and female workers, the levels of skill involved, and so on) but also with the liveliness or otherwise of the surrounding labour market.

Albert J. Mills, reporting on his findings in *New Society*, located 102 distinct occupations between July 1971 and March 1974.[6] 74 of these were in engineering, and they accounted for over ninety per cent of all those employees involved. Engineering is, of course, the largest industry. But since more than half of these sit-ins were among the rash of Lancashire pay disputes of March-June 1972, which were not about redundancy, they were not subject to "wasting away", because they represented a form of strike action in pursuit of demands within continuing industrial relations. Such demands assume that, at the end of a dispute, the entire labour force involved at the beginning will be available to return to normal working.

A Newcastle study, which provides much valuable information about the course of occupations in the North-East,[7] estimates that nationally there were 31 sit-ins or work-ins in 1973, involving over 22,000 workpeople, and 24 occupations in 1974, which again involved 22,000. In 1975 44 occupations were traced by this team, and the workforce participating were estimated to number 21,500. This yields a total of approximately 150,000 workers involved in more than 200 occupations from the beginning of the UCS story until the end of 1975.

By November 1975, the Metra consultancy was able to produce a second report,[8] containing information about sit-ins during the first six months of that year. It had by now become clearly necessary to classify sit-ins, treating separately that group which involved contesting redundancy notices or threats, and that which pursued other disputes on matters of general industrial relations. The first Metra report had predicted, in 1972, a more widespread use of the sit-in as an industrial weapon. The second report confirmed that such an increase had in fact taken place. Using as sources the *Financial Times* and the *Socialist Worker*, the Oxford researchers located 27 sit-ins of one kind or another during the first six months of 1975. Eleven it classified as "defensive" measures against redundancy. 1,200-odd workers were involved in all these taken together. One other action was also initiated against redundancy, but this was styled "assertive" because it had the avowed intention of creating a co-operative replacement enterprise for the old private subsidiary which had collapsed. This case involved 300 people, at the beginning, and 90 at the end. (It was the occupation of the Hull branch of Imperial Typewriters, a subsidiary of Litton Industries, of which more will be said below.)[9] Fifteen of the 1975 sit-ins concerned conventional industrial relations matters, including ten pay claims and a variety of disputes on manning levels, discipline, and control of working arrangements such as safety. Some 12,000 people joined in these fifteen actions, which varied in duration from less than a week up to seven weeks.

Trade Union involvement

Because the UCS initiative quickly received official trade union recognition at the highest level, and because the Engineers' Union was centrally involved in that action, there were few hesitations about extending official recognition to subsequent occupations in the Engineering industry. When Albert Mills completed his enquiry in 1974 he reported:

> "The AUEW is mentioned eight times more than any other union and was involved in almost half the recorded occupations. It was prominent in the first . . . and involved in 25 out of 28 in the next eight months."[10]

Certainly the AEF (as the Engineers' Union then styled itself) was absolutely committed to the first, failed attempt to work on an Liverpool GEC. The local full-time official was a tireless and passionate advocate of the idea of occupying the plant.

Albert Mills seeks to explore the connections between

the Engineers' network and the Communist Party, and offers the suggestion that communists played a major role in initiating occupations.

> "The strength of the Communist Party within the AUEW must have been significant. Many of its leading officials are CP members and a recent estimate put the number of party members at one in 30 . . ."

No doubt the industrial organiser at King Street would like that estimate to be true, but there is every reason to believe it is hopelessly exaggerated. It would mean that the Engineering faction was some 10,000 larger than the entire Party membership. "Officials who were CP members were directly involved in at least two occupations", Albert Mills reports, and there is no reason to doubt this. Full-time officers who were, at the time, communists certainly encouraged occupations on a wide scale during the Engineers' pay-claim. But those initiatives which were taken in the earliest days after the UCS outbreak received, at the beginning, limited coverage in the communist press, as we have reported in the case of Plessey Alexandria. There is some reason to believe to believe that this reflected a certain hesitancy on the part of the Party's organisers, who may have felt their resources to be fully stretched by the work involved in sustaining UCS. Be that as it may, leftists of all kinds were in a minority in most of these actions. Many of their leaders were politically moderate: some were most concerned to differentiate themselves from the political left. While communists played an obvious and effective part in the leadership of the UCS work-in itself, the rush of answering responses around the Clyde was certainly spontaneous, and those union officials who were most actively enthused about repeating the experiment were not notably linked with any particular left-wing current. (Although, of course, in the nature of things, most were supporters or members of the Labour Party.)

Union leaders who publicly identified themselves with work-ins or sit-ins included not only Jack Jones and Hugh Scanlon, but also Jack Peel of the Dyers' and

Bleachers' Union, Clive Jenkins of ASTMS, and Roy Grantham of APEX. Obviously these people represent not only a wide range of different types of trade union, but also the full spectrum of trade union politics. The North-East Trade Union Studies Unit gives the following table of trade union involvement in factory occupations up to 1975.[11]

Trade Union	No. of Occupations in which members were reported as being involved
AUEW	133 (112 Engineering section 21 TASS)
TGWU	21
ASTMS	20
EEPTU	17
APEX	13
UCATT	9
GMWU	8
Sheet Metal Workers	6
SOGAT	4
NATSOPA	4
NGA	4
Boilermakers	4
SLADE	3
NUPE	2
NUJ	2
NUFTO	2

Other unions whose members participated in at least one sit-in or work-in prior to 1976 included the Vehicle Builders, Seamen, Textile Workers, Tailors and Garment Workers, Bakers, Metal Mechanics, Patternmakers and two entertainment unions, the ACTT and NATKE.

Often unions agreed to give full support to their members even before proposed actions had taken place, but these were cases of very complex changes of position within unions once long-term occupations had broken out. It must be remembered that, so convoluted is British Trade Union structure, that few factories are organised by a single union. Many are represented by several different bodies, sometimes demarcated by recruitment of particular skills or trades, but sometimes overlapping and competing with one another. Inter-union disagreements could explain some of the complexities which puzzled commentators on, say, the Briant work-in, in which some print unions changed their policies more than once. Only one union, however, offered outright opposition to a work-in: this was NUFLAT, the footwear union responsible for organising Sexton's factory at Fakenham. The General Secretary wrote to say he could not "condone" the actions of his women members, while the local organiser was reported as telling them "not to be silly girls".

By the time of the second Metra study, this kind of reaction had become virtually inconceivable "although few unions have any formal resolution on sit-ins, most have resolutions opposing redundancies, and without exception the unions will support a redundancy occupation".

In this, the unions might well have been able to call on the testimony of the Metra group itself, because it had reported, in 1972, that occupations afforded five general advantages to the unions, as opposed to other conventional forms of strike action. They gave the unions control of the establishment, putting an absolute impediment in the way of the importation of non-union labour and preventing the removal of equipment. In a sense they minimised the conflict because they obviated the need for pickets of a conventional kind. It was more comfortable for trade unionists to sit inside a plant than to stand outside it. They maintained a high level of morale, since members stayed together and did not drift apart: "it was said of one sit-in that some persons had mixed feelings when it ended because it had provided a satisfying experience in their working lives". Lastly, in struggles against redundancy they were an effective last-ditch resort when otherwise all inducement to negotiate was removed from the employer. One union officer thought that the use of the weapon in wage-claims was unwise, because it guaranteed good plant maintenance, the lack of which might well be a factor in persuading an employer to settle. Other officials thought it unwise to jeopardise public support for right-to-work occupations by indiscriminate use of occupations for other purposes.

Footnotes

1. Graham Chadwick: The Manchester Engineering Sit-ins. In Barratt Brown and Coates: *The Trade Union Register 3*, Spokesman, 1973, p.113 et seq.
2. John Gretton, in *New Society*, 15th June 1972, pp.564-6.
3. See Terry Bishop: *When the Workers take Control*: Personnel Management, March 1973.
4. See *Inside Story*: How Red was Briant Colour? (No.10, August 1973).
5. METRA Consulting Group: *An Analysis of Sit-ins*, London 1972.
6. Albert J. Mills: Factory Work-ins; in *New Society*, 22nd August 1974.
7. North East Trade Union Studies Information Unit: *Workers' Occupations*, 1976 (the Newcastle Study).
8. METRA Consulting Group: *The Worker Sit-in in Britain*, Oxford 1975.
9. See *Why Imperial Typewriters Must Not Close*: IWC Pamphlet No.46, 1975.
10. Op.cit., *New Society*, 22nd August 1974.
11. Newcastle Study, op.cit., pp.95-6.

Appendix: An Employer's Response

The reaction of employers to the development described above was not slow in coming. The following document was prepared by the Employment department at Fords for the briefing of company managers. It was first published in the Bulletin *of the Institute for Workers' Control. Not only does it speak for itself, but it shows how far the unions had come, between 1971 and 1975, towards making factory occupations a standard industrial relations practice.*

The unauthorised occupation of work places and offices is becoming an increasingly popular form of industrial action and can take many forms, ranging from a work-in or sit-in, to marching through a plant, controlling entries and exits, and interfering with the movement of people and materials.

All forms of unauthorised occupation have the same objective: to take physical control of premises and sometimes people, in pursuit of a grievance or demand.

Other forms of industrial action such as strikes or overtime bans lead to loss of production. The occupation of premises has a far worse potential, from interference with equipment and stock to destruction of buildings and machinery and physical violence to persons. In the extreme, e.g. Lip in France, there has been appropriation and sale of the finished product by the occupiers.

Fortunately, EAO experiences with unauthorised occupations have been largely peaceful but this cannot be depended upon for the future. THE KEY TO PREVENTING OR MINIMISING THE EFFECT OF OCCUPATIONS IS TO PLAN PREVENTIVE ACTIONS AND MANAGEMENT RESPONSE BEFORE THE EVENT OCCURS.

Contingency Planning

The following check list is based on experience to date and forms a basis on which detailed plans should be drawn up now against an event occurring in the future. Planning should apply equally to contractors on site as to employees and locations.

Prevention:

Unauthorised occupations can be triggered by:

— lack of communication
— management action seen by employees to be hasty or unfair
— employees feeling they cannot influence events any other way.

It may be possible to prevent an occupation occurring by careful attention in the normal course of work to:

— ensuring good communications with all employees
— considering whether to consult before acting
— considering whether face-to-face contact might not be better than a written statement
— avoiding actions seen to be a "fait accompli"
— avoiding, where possible, confrontations.

Management and supervision should be alert to unusual events occurring which might give early warning of latent trouble building up.

Protection

Check that security arrangements for confidential papers and records are adequate against interference or theft by unauthorised occupiers.

WORK-INS, SIT-INS AND INDUSTRIAL DEMOCRACY

Ensure that vital and highly confidential material is adequately secured in safes or strongrooms. Certified duplicates of vital material (Contracts, Licences, permits etc.) should be banked.

Check security of senior management offices. Are arrangements sufficient to deny access to unauthorised occupiers?

Consider whether the Plant Manager's office and medical department should have more than one means of access.

Check that the public address system can be immobilised so that it cannot be used by unauthorised occupiers.

Ensure adequate perimeter security. Can gates be lifted off their hinges? Is fencing in good condition? Should fencing be reinforced around car/truck parks?

Plan adequate security to deny access to unauthorised occupiers to data processing and computer facilities and telephone exchanges.

Security of the workplace — plan to be able to:

— shut off services, e.g. air, steam, gas, etc.
— immobilise wheeled vehicles, e.g. fork lift trucks
— shut off supplies of food and drink, including vending machines
— make internal concourse areas unusable as gathering places for meetings.

Control and Co-ordination

A senior person (desirably the location manager) to be clearly identified as responsible for all control and co-ordination, both in planning contingency actions and in handling incidents.

There should be a Control Centre to which reports will be made and from which effective co-ordination can be achieved. This Centre should be adequately equipped to allow long-term occupation. Attention should be given to the provision of First Aid equipment, drinking water supply, toilet access etc.

A log book or diary of incidents should be kept as a responsibility of the senior manager having security responsibilities for the location.

Notes should be kept of all incidents and discussions including speeches, ultimatums, threats etc., plus all relevant telephone calls.

Identification should be made of those taking a leading part in any unauthorised occupation and related incidents.

Communication

Every effort should be made to obtain copies of literature, handouts etc., circulated by those involved in an unauthorised occupation.

An occupation should be kept under as much observation as possible without being provocative. All observations are to be referred to the Control Centre for entry in the logbook or diary.

Both senior managers and the Control Centre should have

SPREADING OUT ALL OVER...

telephone lines connected directly to the public system, i.e. not through the internal exchange.

Home telephone numbers should be kept up to date and in the possession of senior managers.

Develop a management communications plan on the "cascade" principle, detailing who 'phones whom, so that management can be rapidly and effectively contacted at home.

Develop a rapid and effective communications plan at work for management and supervision, and for employees, especially those likely to be affected by consequential lay-off, and accredited employee representatives. Consider keeping up to date a set of envelopes pre-addressed to all employees' home address.

Have a plan for communicating with:

— Suppliers — to stop deliveries
— Fire and Police authorities (through the manager having security responsibilities)
— Local public authorities
— Press, radio, etc., (through Public Affairs) — both their approaches to management and management's need to give warning of, for instance, lay-off or shutdown.

Portable loudhailers should be available for management use.

Handling unauthorised occupations

The extreme form of the action means that it may be generated by "unofficial" leaders, rather than by established employee representatives, and for this reason occupations are difficult to deal with.

There are therefore four principles which should be followed in dealing with situations likely to lead to occupations of Company property:

> Prevent it happening by dealing effectively, through normal procedures, with employee grievances.
> *Planning must proceed on developing solutions to the stated grievances — real or imagined.*
> If it does occur, take every possible action to avoid giving in, as concessions merely encourage greater use of this kind of action in the future and undermine the authority of both management and established employee representatives.
> Where "unofficial" leaders are involved, do everything possible to foster the authority and credibility of established employee representatives.

Company experience to date

No common characteristics run through the actions that have occurred on Company property. In the Cologne and Genk incidents employees were sufficiently agitated by their grievance, real or imagined, that unofficial leaders were able to lead them. Specifically, we have had occupations in the following circumstances:

Doncaster: A sit-in following the announced closure of the toolroom and transfer of dies to another location;

Dagenham: A work-in for one day of sewing machinists following their lay-off as a result of the Assembly Plant being laid off;

Dagenham: A mass demonstration in the office block following the laying off of employees several hours after commencement of a night shift;

Cologne: The occupation of Company property following the dismissal of several hundred foreign workers returning late to work (by several days) after shutdown;

Genk: A sit-in following the disciplinary dismissal of an employee representative.

Legal Aspects

The two most important considerations arising are whether or not Police intervention should be requested, and what should be the role of Company personnel.

While it would be prudent to advise the civil authority when an occupation has occurred, police intervention should usually be requested only when there is evidence of, or danger of, assaults on persons or damage to or theft of property. It is quite probable that an occupation will attract militants, and one of their objectives may well be to provoke confrontation in order to achieve their own aims.

However, there may be occasions when earlier intervention by the civil authority can prevent an incident occurring, and such preventive action may be indicated.

Company personnel should not be used to protect persons or property if this puts them in danger themselves.

The type of evidence required by a Court of Law in assaults on persons or damage to property varies, but principally depends on the statements of witnesses, whilst other evidence such as photographs or tape recordings may be supportive. However, it has to be recognised that the action of Company personnel taking photographs or recordings may well be provocative.

Management action during unauthorised occupations
1. To minimise escalation

Occupations, by their nature, are likely to be contagious and it is essential that management take prompt action as early as possible to avoid escalation.

Employees taking part should be induced to start work or to leave the premises.

If this is not possible, then they should be induced to leave their workplace for a more secluded area such as a canteen or locker room.

The entry of outsiders should be prevented, particularly as these may well be external militants. Press, radio, etc., should only be admitted when duly authorised in consultation with Public Affairs and at the discretion of the location manager.

Management must communicate fully and promptly with all those not involved so as to keep them fully in the picture.

2. To protect Company property

Evidence suggests that damage to Company property is not an objective of Company employees involved in occupations, although it might be an objective of outside persons who become involved.

Management and Supervision should only act in their normal role of collecting facts and making reasonable attempts to restore work. They may witness and note actions by occupiers for notification to the Control Centre, but they should not go beyond this.

Only accustomed levels of management and supervision should be involved with the occupiers. For example, the sudden arrival of senior management and Security personnel could encourage the occupiers to believe that they were achieving their objectives.

3. To avoid violence

It is principally the responsibility of the Company to ensure that the situation remains peaceful, although it may become necessary to request the assistance of the civil authorities. But note that while the civil authority will intervene at the request of the Company, they may thereafter handle the situation in a manner that, and for as long as, they see fit.

Company Security personnel should continue to be used, in both occupied and unoccupied areas, to protect Company property and to prevent the entry of unauthorised personnel. When their presence is impractical in the occupied areas every effort should be made to ensure continued operation of fire control duties.

No firm guidance can be given on the disconnection of water, power and light, and the immobilisation of wheeled vehicles. This will depend upon safety aspects and on the risk of escalation. Consideration should be given to disconnecting telephones available to unauthorised occupiers. The question of whether or not the Company continues the provision of normal canteen facilities will depend upon the circumstances at the time. It may well be that the provision of such facilities will have a positive effect in reducing the possibility of escalation.

Employees should not continue to work in areas near to an occupation.

It is likely to be inflammatory to use the plant public address system to address the occupiers.

Experience in the past indicates that members of management attempting to address occupiers may be shouted down, and therefore a portable loud hailer should be available for use.

4. To restore normal working

The occupiers are most likely to be open to reason in the initial stages of their action, before they become committed and before external militants get involved. Therefore management should work as speedily and effectively as early as possible to obtain a return to work. Management should avoid if possible dealing with unofficial leaders.

If the incident does not come to an end, then it will ultimately be necessary to contact the leaders of the occupation, directly or indirectly, to see what could be done to restore normal working without negotiating on the grievances.

Industrial Relations Staff
EAO
February 20, 1975

Chapter VIII

The TUC takes its stand

From the beginning, official trade union support was generously provided to the sit-in movement. We have already documented key practical instances of this, but now we shall consider the policy conclusions which were drawn from all these events by the TUC itself.

At one level, the 1971 upsurge provoked its own response from the unions. But this was powerfully reinforced by two proposals from the European Economic Community. The first of these was a proposed statute for a "European Company" which had limited scope, but which preoccupied the Council of Ministers during the years following the UCS work-in. It allowed for a modified version of the German system of co-determination, and was to be a European formula for company constitution, optionally available to enterprises operating anywhere within the Community, alongside existing national company laws. The second was the draft fifth directive on company law, which offered broadly "German" and "Dutch" variants of workers' involvement on company supervisory boards. Both had to be taken seriously, because of the avid support for the EEC by the Heath administration. For this reason, the TUC prepared its report on Industrial Democracy, which we have discussed elsewhere at some length. This began with a consideration of the evolution of collective bargaining, and quickly registered its own entirely supportive analysis of the sit-in movement in this context:

WORK-INS, SIT-INS AND INDUSTRIAL DEMOCRACY

"Trade Union Tactics: Sit-ins and Work-ins"

12 Significance must also be attached to the adoption of new or revised forms of industrial action by trade unions, in particular in the face of managerial decisions involving closures and large-scale redundancies. The UCS work-in and the subsequent sit-ins and similar actions involved workers already employed at an establishment taking control over that establishment, with the intention of obtaining a change in management decisions. Four types of such action can be distinguished: (a) work-ins; (b) sit-ins over major managerial decisions; (c) collective bargaining sit-ins; (d) and tactical sit-ins.

13 The most significant instance of the work-in was at Upper Clyde Shipbuilders. The UCS work-in began on July 30, 1971. Its aim was the retention of all four yards, with the full eight-and-a-half thousand workforce. Its defining feature was the refusal of the employees to accept redundancy notices or to register at the employment exchange. The work-in formally ended on October 10, 1972 when the Co-ordinating Committee members returned to their trades after three yards began operating under Govan Shipbuilders and the fourth yard under Marathon Manufacturing. There have been relatively few real work-ins besides the UCS example though similar tactics have been used at Sexton's Leather Workshop in Fakenham, Norfolk, and at Briant Colour Printing.

14 "Sit-ins" against closures took place, involving workers taking complete control of the factories but not carrying on working. These occupations thus combined the characteristics of a strike with those of a factory takeover. Usually the issue over which action was taken was the closure of a relatively isolated, and relatively peripheral plant by larger combines. Four such sit-ins that were wholly or partly successful were: Plessey (Alexandria), Fisher-Bendix, Allis Chalmers, and the former BLMC Thorneycroft factory at Basingstoke. There was also a spate of sit-in strikes as part of the 1972 engineering industry dispute. In some instances, what might be called a "tactical" sit-in has been used, as part of a wider strategy rather than as the major strategy in itself. This can range from a half-hour sit-down at a production line to a sit-in of a few days, without taking over the factory completely. Quite often instances of this type of immediate action by workers at the shop-floor go unreported. In addition, there has recently been the development by unions of other approaches for resisting projected closures. Purchase by workers' co-operatives has been one of these, and variants have been seen at the former Norton Villiers Triumph factory at Meriden, and at the former Scottish Daily Express."

Speaking to this Report at the 1974 Congress, Len

Murray called for the extension of the "status quo" principle in procedural agreements, "so that major decisions are made by agreement instead of management trying to impose them", and for greater accountability.

The issue, he said "is how we can bring all major policies in industry within the area of joint regulation". This was to be accomplished by extending collective bargaining, and also by company law reform which would reinforce this. Some delegates found this an ambiguous package, and the Constructional Engineers put up a composite motion to insist that

> "any extension of trade union participation in industrial management shall be, and shall be seen to be, an extension of collective bargaining, and shall in no sense compromise the unions' role . . ."

This provoked Mr Murray, in replying, to insist that just as Marx stood Hegel on his feet, the TUC were attempting to stand the German system on its feet "by emphasising trade union election, trade union accountability, only and exclusively through trade union machinery as such". The Congress then carried both the General Council's *Report* and the apprehensive composite, together with a parallel motion on the democratisation of nationalised industries.

It was not until 1975 that Congress debated "work-ins" and factory occupations in their own right. SLADE, the Printworkers' union, moved that

> "Congress recognises that the occupation of plants and factories, sometimes including the maintenance of work within those plants, has become an accepted feature of the struggle by working people to prevent closures, unemployment, and loss of job opportunities.
>
> Congress calls for changes in the law which would enable such occupations to be treated as accepted forms of industrial action with immunity from legal proceedings.
>
> Congress particularly draws attention to the problems arising from merchant ships being homes as well as workplaces for seafarers."

The purpose of this motion, said its mover, Mr J.A. Jackson, was "to oppose any move to make work-ins illegal" and to free occupations from the threat of prosecutions for criminal trespass or conspiracy to trespass. We shall return to this issue later. The interesting point about Mr Jackson's argument was that he derived it not from the experience of UCS or other sit-ins, but from his own work-experience in the printing trade, raked over and often subsequently re-raked by convulsive technological changes:

> "We are one of the craft unions in the printing industry and, as some of our colleagues will tell you, more crafty than some. Our part of the industry and indeed the industry itself used to be labour-intensive. Our members, men and women, did the work, provided the know-how and the skill to produce the job. Indeed, without the people with that know-how and skill the job could not be produced. In the unions, certainly in our union, if we controlled the members, the labour, then we controlled production and we had a bargaining position with the boss and with the employer. In recent years our industry like most, we believe, has become much more capital-intensive and less labour-intensive. We have had tremendous productivity increases. Machines, sophisticated equipments and techniques, very expensive, have come in. They have not only increased productivity, but they have supplied that skill, that production which was previously the prerogative of the craftsmen. Also, because of the increase in productivity and the more specialised techniques, production has become more specialised. A trade house might do a bit of a job, a firm somewhere else might finish the job and it is difficult on occasions to tell where a job starts and where it ends.
>
> But the point for us in the trade unions in the printing industry is that it is no longer true that if we control the labour we necessarily control production. On the contrary, the lesson we have learned more and more is that to maintain our bargaining position with the employer, the owner, we not only have to control the labour. We have to control the machines, the sophisticated equipments which are giving our industry so much higher productivity than it had before. Our industry, like most others in recent years, has worshipped at the altar of higher productivity. Like most other industries, we went along with that, saying that if we could increase our production more and more, do much more that we did the year before and even more than we did the year before that, at the end of the day we would all be better off. We have found that that does not always work out. As most of our colleagues here will know, it only works out when you not only produce more but you manage to sell more as well. Our experience is that we have produced a great deal more, more

often than the employer has managed to sell, a great deal more, and we have outstripped the market. This has led to firms combining one with the other, the creation of groups, and on from that the rationalisation of production to cut it down to bring it more into line with what they can sell, with what the market will bear. And it brings closures. We have had our share in the printing industry and sometimes we feel it has been more than our share."

This is a classic statement of a case which has its analogues in dozens of other sectors, and which especially hits those traditionally white-collar tasks in which computers and modern electronics are displacing all kinds of intermediary occupations. This point was emphasised in the Congress debate by Mr Clay, of the Technical Administrative and Supervisory Section of the AUEW.

"There is another aspect. It has been mentioned by our colleague from SLADE. As technological advance in industry continues, as sophisticated machines are introduced, often-computer-controlled, many workers and especially white collar workers are finding that if it is necessary to have a strike, whether it be about money or conditions, it is better sometimes to stay on the premises to have the strike, to make sure that machines cannot be operated by management, by non-union labour, by blacklegs. I can tell you that many disputes that we now have in TASS are being conducted on the premises."

The SLADE motion was carried, after Harry Urwin, speaking on behalf of the General Council, had committed the TUC to opposing the package of proposals by the Law Commission, which later became known as the "Criminal Trespass Bill". This contentious initiative passed into law as the Criminal Law Act 1977. TUC opposition, Mr Urwin explained, was based on the grounds that the new measures "would substantially widen the areas of Criminal Trespass and bring it more prominently into the area of industrial disputes" by creating a new offence of unlawfully failing to leave a property after being ordered to do so by a person entitled to occupation. "That is" said Mr Urwin, "the employer could order you to leave without a Court Order, and if you did not it would be an offence".

The effect of the 1975 debate was thus twofold. In respect of trespass, it confirmed the TUC view that this was an inappropriate concept in matters of employment and industrial relations: while in its general implications it made clear the overwhelming and rooted support of trade unions for the right of factory occupations when other means of protest were inadequate.

Appendix: The Criminal Law Act

The Criminal Law Act, 1977, known to its critics as the Criminal Trespass Law, gave rise to a widespread campaign of opposition, much of which concerned the defence of the right to undertake work-ins and sit-ins. It was feared that the Act would be invoked against workers who were occupying, or threatening to occupy, their factories or offices. In fact, since the Act came into force late in 1977 there do not appear to have been any cases of its use in industrial disputes, at least insofar as court proceedings are concerned. But there have apparently been cases when police have turned up at occupations, or incipient occupations, and given the impression that they were about to enforce the Criminal Law Act. This has involved a large measure of bluff, and in at least one case police have subsequently denied that they had intended to invoke this Act, claiming instead that they were using other powers.

The complexities and ambiguities of this kind of hassle are manifold, and for this reason the TUC prepared a special document, A5 of its Industrial Relations Bulletin, 1978, to elucidate the meaning of the (then recently new) Act. This document provides a clear exposition of the problems.

On December 1, 1977, the criminal trespass provisions of the Criminal Law Act 1977 came into force. These provisions have possible implications for legitimate trade union activities including factory occupations and work-ins. The criminal trespass laws do not make the occupation of factories or plants, in themselves, illegal — but they make illegal a number of actions which could occur (or be alleged to occur) during work-ins or sit-ins.

The criminal trespass laws make it a criminal offence:

  i. to use or threaten violence to persons or property to gain entrance

to premises (whether or not residential) knowing that someone is on the premises opposed to entry;
ii. to be on any premises without permission with a 'weapon of offence';
iii. to resist or obstruct a bailiff enforcing a court order.

At the outset, it should be made clear that the criminal trespass provisions do not replace, *but are in addition to*, the existing civil court procedures for the eviction of trespassers.

These criminal trespass provisions are not the only criminal laws relating to trespass. For example, the Forcible Entry Acts of 1381, 1429, 1588 and 1623 dealt with these matters although they had been judicially discredited and unused for many years, and are now repealed. In addition, the Sheriffs Act of 1887 makes it a criminal offence to obstruct a sheriff who is carrying out a court order, although this Act has been almost unused until very recently. These new criminal trespass provisions do not apply to Scotland or Northern Ireland, only to England and Wales.

This article will examine the background history to these new laws and in particular, the General Council's efforts to change them; the criminal trespass provisions in detail and their possible implications for factory occupations and police involvement; and the penalties which may result upon conviction under the new offences.

Background

In 1975 the Trades Union Congress carried a resolution which called for changes in the law which would exempt factory and plant occupations from liability to legal proceedings. The General Council pressed the Employment Secretary to introduce such legal immunities but he refused to extend trade union immunities for a number of reasons which included the Parliamentary situation at that time. Subsequently in March 1976, the Law Commission published a report *Conspiracy and Criminal Law Reform*, which contained, inter alia, a number of new criminal offences relating to trespass which would include factory and plant occupations. The General Council, mindful of the 1975 Congress Resolution, continued to press the Government for factory or plant work-ins or sit-ins by trade unionists in contemplation or furtherance of a trade dispute to be excluded from any trespass law. However the Government introduced a Criminal Law Bill into the House of Lords which contained, in largely unchanged form, the Law Commission's proposals on criminal trespass. While the General Council welcomed other parts of the Bill which restricted the common law offence of conspiracy and the maximum sentences which could be imposed under conspiracy charges, it firmly opposed the criminal trespass provisions of the Bill in detailed correspondence and in a series of meetings with the Home Secretary.

During these discussions, the General Council obtained a number of minor amendments in the original criminal trespass provisions, including protection for trade unionists engaged in occupations where their place of work was also their residence and the restriction to uniformed police officers of the power of arrest under these provisions. The Bill received its Royal Assent in August 1977 and the criminal trespass provisions came into effect on December 1, 1977.

The Criminal Trespass Provisions

Part 2 of the Criminal Law Act which contains the criminal trespass provisions, creates five new offences. One of these is concerned with domestic premises and another with the premises of foreign embassies; attention will be focused on the remaining three offences.

1. To use or threaten violence to persons or property for the purpose of securing entry into any premises — whether or not residential — knowing that someone else is on the premises opposed to entry (Section 6 of the Criminal Law Act 1977).

This offence has three elements, namely — entry, someone opposing entry, and the use or threat of violence, and all three of them must be present or have occurred before a prosecution can be secured. "Entry" means the act of entering and in most cases workers already will have entered the employers premises, but the law is unclear as to whether the act of entering separate parts of a large factory building e.g. the management offices, would constitute entry. However the entry of physically separate buildings on a site would constitute "entry" under the Act. For the "opposed entry" requirement, it would be sufficient for someone to state "you can't come in". It is more difficult to assess what constitutes a threat of violence but possibly a verbal threat or a physical gesture which implied violence would suffice. As to whether large number of pickets would constitute a threat of violence, in 1973 the Conservative Attorney-General, Peter Rawlinson, stated that "sheer numbers attending, can, of itself, constitute intimidation". The present Attorney-General, Mr Sam Silkin, affirmed in 1977 that in his opinion he does not consider sheer numbers of people would be sufficient in themselves to constitute intimidation but it is not clear what interpretation will be placed on this by prosecuting authorities.

2. To be on any premises without permission with a weapon of offence (Section 8 of the Criminal Law Act 1977).

There are two main points here: first, that a weapon of offence can mean any article with which someone *intends* to cause injury or incapacitate another person. Courts in the past have found that banners, placards, shoes, bunches of keys and other personal effects have constituted offensive weapons. In the context of factory occupations, tools and workplace implements could easily be construed to mean offensive weapons: however, the prosecuting authorities would need to show that there was an intention to use them as offensive weapons. Second, the police are allowed to enter and search premises and to make arrests if they reasonably suspect any of these new offences to have been committed. This means that for the reason that they reasonably suspect that offensive weapons were present, the police have sufficient authority to enter a plant where there is an occupation or work-in and make arrests. Normally, the police are only allowed to enter, search and make arrests where the offences are very serious and carry maximum sentences of five years' jail. However, the Criminal Law Act gives police these powers to search and arrest in connection with criminal trespass offences whose maximum sentences are six months' imprisonment.

3. To resist or intentionally obstruct a bailiff or Sheriff enforcing a possession order (Section 10 of the Criminal Law Act 1977).

This new law makes it an offence to resist eviction, and to refuse to move barricades could be construed as obstructing a court officer under this section.

Under past and existing civil law, if an employer wanted to regain possession of an occupied factory, he has to apply to the civil courts for a possession order which is served by a bailiff or a sheriff. (For premises which a rateable value of over £2,000 the sheriff is used and under £2,000, a bailiff.) This procedure is a civil procedure and the police are not usually involved unless there is a breach of peace.

For the past year or so, there have been a number of prosecutions for obstructing a sheriff under the Sheriffs Act including prosecutions against a number of underground construction workers who occupied an underground shaft in North London during an industrial dispute.

Penalties

The maximum penalty for the first and third of the above offences (i.e. entry with violence, and resisting a court officer) is six months in prison or £1,000 or both. The maximum penalty for the second offence (i.e. trespass with an offensive weapon) is three months in jail or £1,000 or both. There is no right to jury trial with any of the above offences: they all are to be tried in magistrates' courts only.

In other parts of the Criminal Law Act, there are large increases in the maximum fines for offences with which pickets and demonstrators are commonly charged. The maximum fine for obstructing a police constable in the course of his duty is increased from £20 to £200. Similarly the maximum fine for assaulting a police officer, or for conduct likely to cause a brech of peace is increased from £100 to £1,000.

WORK-INS, SIT-INS AND INDUSTRIAL DEMOCRACY

TUC Action

During 1977 and 1978, the General Council have been urging the Home Secretary to exclude trade disputes from the scope of the Criminal Law Act and to amend the criminal trespass provisions. The General Council have been concerned that the manner in which prosecuting authorities and the courts could interpret the Act could lead to curbs on legitimate trade union action in trade disputes, particularly in relation to factory occupations. The Home Secretary replied that in his view the Act should have no effect on peaceful industrial action or other forms of peaceful demonstration. Pressed by the General Council for further assurances, the Home Secretary has stated that his view on the lack of dangers of the Act to trade union activities has been clearly communicated to chief officers of police. According to the Home Secretary there has been no evidence of abuse of the criminal trespass provisions nor of the Act having unfortunate effects in industrial disputes. However, should disturbing developments occur in relation to peaceful industrial action, the Home Secretary has said that he will be willing to meet the General Council to discuss the need for amending legislation.

In May the General Council issued a circular (No.201(1977-78)) to all affiliated organisations requesting them to report to the TUC any instances where the criminal trespass provisions have been used during peaceful industrial action.

Chapter IX

A Rebirth of Co-operation?

Although the creation of workers' producer co-operatives came relatively late, arguments about whether co-operative production might be possible broke out in many of the earlier sit-ins, and were often discouraged by the political groupings who flocked around to offer advice and support. It may seem a "natural" response to an active trade unionist, once he has begun to doubt the permanence of the relationship of employer-employee itself, rather than raising the simpler problem of shifting given terms of employment in his favour, to begin to consider some form of localised or co-operative self-management.[1] "Why don't you keep it?" was a question asked all over the country, and not only by the children of the Liverpool Free School, who had visited the occupied Fisher-Bendix factory early in 1972. Factory occupations encouraged precisely such questioning. As they became more and more common, the questions they posed to their participants became more insistent.

The first modern occupation to result in the formation of a co-operative producer's association was a special case. At Fakenham, in Norfolk, a small group of women leather workers, belonging to a very conservative trade union, the National Union of Footwear, Leather and Allied Trades, took over their little factory in order to resist its closure. After a 17 week long work-in, they were able to secure financial backing from the Scott Bader Commonwealth (a successful common ownership organisation operating a chemical factory at

Wellingborough) and to establish their own self-managed company in new premises.[2] During the occupation the women manufactured suede dresses and handbags which they were able to sell through volunteers, many of whom came forward from the Women's Liberation Movement. In spite of strong hostility from the Executive Committee of their trade union,[3] and a churlish response from their local official, they received considerable support from their fellow-members, and were able to secure publicity on a national scale.

The capital requirements of such a restricted enterprise were quite modest and well within the means of an established organisation such as Scott Bader. The initial loan given to the women was £2,500. As the new co-operative extended itself, the workforce grew from 10 to 30 and Scott Bader successively provided further loans, totalling £10,000 over three years. After an initial experiment in diversification, the women took on a professional manager and agreed to concentrate on manufacturing uppers for shoes, and this degree of specialisation brought them into considerable difficulty when the shoe industry entered another recession in 1975. In the end, they went under. But the Fakenham experiment helped to draw attention to a time-honoured prescription for industrial democracy: and even in work-ins and sit-ins where the co-operative option was far more difficult to realise, there were voices raised in its favour. For instance, at the Briant Colour Printing work-in, which attracted widespread support for what became a very militant dispute, there were apparently insistent calls to explore the possibility of establishing a co-operative,[4] which were voted down on the recommendation of the work-in's leaders. Here the protective practices which were the very foundation of printing unionism deviously clashed with the co-operative option, which was bound to be interpreted in some unions as an attempt to cut corners.

At Leadgate Engineering, at Durham in the North of England, another co-operative (known as Nightsbridge

Ltd.) was established, with the help of the parent company which had been compelled to reconsider its original decision to close its Durham plant by the resultant six-month six-in. This company, Stibbe & Co, was a hosiery firm based in Leicester, which controlled a number of subsidiary plants engaged in the manufacture of hosiery machinery. It had hoped to transfer the machinery from its Durham factory to another closer to HQ. When it agreed to recognise the rights of the labour force (which it had unsuccessfully declared redundant) to form a co-operative, it negotiated a contract under which it would agree to purchase the hosiery machinery by the new enterprise.

"Leadgate", wrote Bel Mooney,[5] "is a classic case of closure, confrontation and sit-in at a small engineering works near Durham, in a depressed area where unemployment runs at 8 per cent. But at Leadgate the industrial action of the Seventies has been given a unique twist . . .

"From the moment Leadgate Engineering opened its doors to manufacture industrial knitting machines until its closure three years later the prospects for the Leicester-based parent company, G. Stibbe & Co, and therefore (it seemed) for the workers — many of them ex-miners — looked good. Stibbe bought the 10-acre site from the National Coal Board for a rock-bottom price of £75,000. With the help of £145,000 in government grants and subsidies for regional development, machinery worth about £130,000 was installed, and on 1st July 1969 Leadgate Engineering Ltd was in business. Employment rose to 306, an apprentices' training school was established, and by March 1972 the branch was showing profits. A senior executive of Stibbe rapturously described Leadgate as a 'success story for the group' — and the group was doing very nicely. In 1971 Stibbe's group sales were £11,878,000, and pre-tax profits stood at £1,264,000 — enabling the chairman, Mr Paul Stibbe to up his pay from £9,203 to £18,830. Average pay at Leadgate was £38 a week."

The ex-miners who staffed the plant were willing workers, and the AUEW convenor, Fred Conlyon, who played an active part in the formation of the new co-operative, described the move from the pits to the factory as "like moving from hell to heaven". For this reason, "the workers at Leadgate were more than usually willing to co-operate with management. Stibbe showed his appreciation by arriving early on the morning of 5th June 1972, and informing their local director, Mr Reed, that the branch was to be closed . . . What shocked both local management and men, apart from the seeming pointlessness of the closure (when £3,000 had been spent on improvements the week before), was the fact that there had been no warning, no consultation. By way of explanation, Stibbe said that due to a recession in the industry orders for new machines had been postponed — not cancelled.

"The men at Leadgate might have been even angrier had they known at the time what they later discovered — that 300 jobs are nothing beside a board-room squabble. In April director Hugh Stibbe had attacked his brother, chairman Paul Stibbe, for the way he was running the company. In May the *Daily Telegraph* was commenting: 'Strife-torn industries do not usually make the best investments, but there must be a strong case for investing in the shares of G. Stibbe'. In June Leadgate was closed, and Hugh Stibbe, head of the 'rival' faction in the boardroom, said: 'This goes to prove that the company is not being run by competent management'. Mr William Reed, who had just put his case against Stibbe in the hands of a solicitor, still believes that the real story has not been fully disclosed."

Stibbe's were careful, as Bel Mooney pointed out: "By closing Leadgate and opening a new branch in an area of high unemployment, valuable machines that had been bought with the aid of government grants could be transferred. It takes little imagination to see that Stibbe might be not 100 miles away from saving money. They still say that it was regrettable, though they knew that other small engineering firms in the area were likely to close and that even the position of British Steel, the largest employer in the area, was precarious. It was inevitable, unavoidable business, they say. And as usual, they assumed that their workers would see the difficulty of their position".

That was how, in July, 100 Leadgate workers began their six-month sit-in.

Gradually their numbers diminished, just as they did in so many other long-term occupations. But there were still 30 workers out of the original resistance complement of 100 when the new co-operative was formed, once Stibbe had agreed to negotiate a settlement.

The contract which Leadgate's workers were ultimately able to negotiate with their reluctant "parent" Company was remarkably similar in effect to the earlier proposal of the Guild Socialist Movement, the "collective contract", under which work-groups were to become autonomous and self-regulating, whilst remaining collectively tied to an employer who treated with them, as a group for the delivery of a specific product or service. The Nightbridge co-op was given a loan of £3,000 by Stibbe's, in addition to a guarantee of work. This loan bore no interest for the first three months. At the end of a year, the co-op repaid its debt, took on additional staff, and paid average wages of £30 a week. It began to negotiate for a lease on the site. Then, a casualty of the three-day week and its resultant shortages, it closed. Even after this trauma, it reopened, and carried a staff of 50 until late 1975. It survived the cancellation of the basic Stibbe contract, to founder in the engineering recession.

At Fakenham, on the other hand, a small work-group in a labour-intensive enterprise, could relatively easily make the transition to fully independent co-operative self-management.

In general, capital shortage is usually a sufficient handicap to prevent more substantial enterprises from continuing production on a co-operative basis after closure by their former owners: but small handicrafts business and combines of highly-skilled professional or technically qualified people are ideally suited to this kind of development. Little though they may be in scale, they can exercise a powerful leavening influence on the conventionally managed industry surrounding them, provided only that their practitioners maintain their active links with the trade union and labour movements which sustained their initiation.

The real breakthrough in experiment with co-operative forms of organisation, however, came with the election of the February 1974 Labour Government, which brought Tony Benn back to the office of Secretary of State for Industry. Here he inherited a variety of problems of factory closure, in a general liquidity crisis which was rapidly inducing bankruptcies in numerous parts of British manufacturing industry. At the time he came to office, there was a major dispute running in the motor cycle industry, where the Norton Villiers Triumph factory at Meriden was under occupation by at least 250 of the original 1,750 workers who had been declared redundant in a programme of reorganisation initiated by the owners of the plant, who were concentrating motor cycle production in the Birmingham factory at Small Heath. Meriden was soon to be joined by other occupations. We have discussed these events in detail, elsewhere.[6]

In July of that year, 1,200 workers at the former Fisher-Bendix factory at Merseyside, which had already been the scene of that prolonged sit-in in 1972, and which had resulted in a temporarily successful rescue operation, found their plant once again on the edge of disaster. They were informed that extensive lay-offs were necessary and that a maximum of 450 jobs could be rescued. Refusing to accept this kind of surgery, they once again occupied the factory and brought the question to the attention of the Industry Minister.[7] Earlier, in March, the offices of the *Scottish Daily Express* in Glasgow had been closed by the proprietors, Beaverbrook Newspapers, in order to concentrate their efforts on extending the sales of the English editions. 1,800 workers were made redundant, and a thousand of them voted to sit-in.[8] Approaches to Mr Peter Shore, the Secretary for Trade in their newly-elected government, did not succeed in saving the newspaper as it stood, but did elicit a promise that the government would look at proposals for a workers' co-operative, which might be able to produce a Scottish daily newspaper in the abandoned plant.

After extensive arguments within the government, Tony Benn was able to persuade it to endorse plans to finance workers' co-operatives in each of these three enterprises. The government agreed to lend £3.9m to the former Fisher-Bendix (IPD) factory, which was to resume operations under the name of the Kirkby Manufacturing & Engineering Company. Of this sum, £1.8m was needed to pay off the Receiver in order to clear the liabiities of the old company. The government also agreed to put up almost £5m for the Meriden motor cycle factory, and to offer £1.75m to the workers' co-operative at what was to become the *Scottish Daily News*, on condition that they raised the balance of the necessary capital. £250,000 had already been collected in personal contributions from the redundant workers, who contributed their severance pay. Half-a-million pounds had to be raised in unsecured loans, and £775,000 from secured loans.

After considerable difficulties each of these co-operatives was successful in establishing itself, although the life of the *Scottish Daily News* was very short, and the KME concern was to go under in 1978, after a prolonged struggle against capital starvation. None of three Government-funded bodies became registered under the legislation governing the formation of co-operative societies for a variety of technical and legal reasons. All chose instead to register as companies under the Companies Act, and provided themselves with statutes, Memoranda and Articles of Association and, where appropriate, trust deeds, which enjoined the strictest participating democracy.

The brief concession to co-operative ideals by the Department of Industry came to an end in 1975, with the victory of the "yes" lobby in the Referendum on membership of the European Economic Community. Once Britain was apparently securely joined to the Common Market, Harold Wilson carried through a cold purge of his cabinet, and moved Tony Benn sideways to the Energy portfolio. Eric Varley took over responsibility for the Industry Department, and this guaranteed that there would be no headline-shaking experiments in producer co-operation.[9] More: it also guaranteed that the existing co-ops, which had been a severe humiliation to departmental officials, would be held on a very tight financial string. The remarkable fact was not that two of the three were choked, but that the process took so long to accomplish. Of course, reversal of policy on this matter was only part of a much more profound shift away from the interventionist commitments of the Labour Party's 1974 Manifesto, which resulted in the blocking of planning agreements, the hampering of the National Enterprise Board, and the gutting of the Industrial Democracy pledges which culminated in the Bullock Report's long wait for further and further measures of dilution and final non-implementation.

But the U-turn by the Wilson administration became plain in the case of Imperial Typewriters, which, in January 1975, closed its two plants in Leicester and Hull. In violation of all written codes, and every custom of "good industrial relations", the owners of these factories, the giant American transnational, Litton Industries, made a surprise announcement of complete closedown, on the Friday afternoon of January 17th, only three days after shop stewards in Hull had been told there was no cause for panic, and that they should "disregard rumours of difficulties". Litton insisted from the beginning that they had no intention of seeking Government aid to remain in production. The evidence seemed to show that their takeover of English typewriter production had been a classic ploy to secure market control, and it is hard to believe that there had been any serious intention of maintaining longterm productive capacity. Once markets were assured, Litton-made machines from Germany were to fill the gap left by the collapse of the British factories.

The TGWU, alongside ASTMS and the AUEW in Hull, occupied the Hull plant. They called for a through investigation into the background of the closure, and at the same time sought to be either nationalised or funded for co-operative production. In questioning the company's intention, they showed a realistic awareness of the difficulties of dealing with transnational operations.

"Litton Industries — a major US multinational company with world sales of £1,000 million in 1973, and listed 46th in size of US owned companies — took over Imperial typewriters, an old-established British company, in 1966. During the same period, it expanded its ownership of typewriter manufacturing throughout the world, including plants in Germany and Japan. Typewriters were seen as one of its major growth sectors. In at least one case, the acquisition of Triumph-Adler, one of two major producers in Germany, Litton was indicted under anti-trust laws in the USA, though the case has not been settled. By whatever means, Litton acquired control of 30 per cent of world typewriter production.

Litton asserts that its British operations at Imperial factories have consistently made losses, and cites a figure of £5m loss over the past two years. In the case of the Hull factory at least, the major part of its production is exported to the United States. Indeed, the reason given for the original purchase of the English company was that Litton's home plant at Hartford, Connecticut, could not compete with low-cost imports. We know that, in addition to the English, German and Japanese subsidiaries of Litton, there has been recent development of productive capacity in low labour cost countries such as Portugal, Singapore, and Brazil, though we are not at this stage able to affirm that these are Litton factories.

What we need to know in this connection is the transfer-pricing policy of the company, between its various subsidiaries, and particularly for imports of machines into the USA from its overseas factories. It is quite possible that wholesale import prices into America were kept artificially low, and that this could account for the scale of Imperial's losses since Litton acquired our factories. With the onset of the domestic recession in the US market, Litton was in a position to choose which of its overseas subsidiaries should be axed. Consequently, Imperial is probably a victim of a purely company-oriented decision bearing no relation to British national economic interest. It is therefore important to investigate the transfer-pricing policy of the company. If the English losses are explainable in this way — or even partially explainable — then the case that our factories are inevitably loss-making and inefficient is far from established. Without this information, we are not disposed to accept the company's figures at their face value.

We also need to investigate the company's policy in another respect. There are a range of related products which can be produced by a modern office-machine company, including not only typewriters, but also calculating machines and other items of office equipment. This group of products uses inter-changeable parts and components, which are all made of similar materials. Considerable economies are available to a company which diversifies its products in these circumstances, and diversification is a normal method employed by an intelligent management to safeguard against the collapse of the markets for particular products and to exploit technological developments. A multinational company may arrange this product-mix on a multinational scale, leaving national subsidiaries dependent on a narrow range of products. We think this is the case with Imperials. The Hull factory is entirely dependent on typewriter production which is technologically the weaker end of the product range, and particularly on the manual model, less advanced than the electrical typewriter. We have some evidence from managers in Hull that, if the factory were allowed to diversify, to add another product to its range, and to recruit about 600 additional workers, it could operate at a profit.

We also have evidence, that we hope to develop, showing some sections of management in the company to be deficient, particularly on the sales and technical side.

These factors represent at least prima facie grounds for questioning whether the plant is inevitably loss-making. To substantiate these points, we need:

  i. access to the Litton accounts, and assistance to complete a study of possible transfer-pricing effects on the English accounts;
  ii. a detailed analysis of world trade in typewriters and office machinery, including statistics of exports and imports between major producing and consuming countries, broken down into figures for whole machines, and components, for portable, office model, manual and electrical typewriters, calculating machines, etc.
  iii. a study of the viability of diversification of products in the

English factories;
iv. an opportunity to examine and report on the management structure and efficient of the English operations."[10]

Pending such an examination, the TGWU called for a stay of execution, if necessary after Government intervention, for maintenance of the workforce while feasibility studies were carried out, and for a complex re-appraisal based on:

"i. doubts about the production and marketing policies of Litton, and the need to assess losses, and potential profitability, by other criteria than those used by the company.
ii. the possibility of import control, and export finance, to enable Imperials to continue its contribution to the Balance of Payments. The certainty of worsening Balance of Payments which would follow closure.
iii. the company's neglect of diversification, and the possibility of developing new products.
iv. the possibility of releasing hitherto untapped resources of human motivation and worker participation in management and performance.
v. the need to explore new markets at least for the duration of the US recession.
vi. the social cost-benefit dimension which, in this preliminary survey, suggests that government assistance and the maintenance of production could be a net benefit.
vii. the possibility that the acquisition of the physical assets of the company need not be prohibitively expensive.
viii. the contribution which governments have already made to the economy of Imperials through tariff concessions, etc'."[11]

But although feasibility studies were in fact begun, and the workers spent many weeks in the silent buildings of their Hull factory, their initiative was doomed. Working without proper tools, they designed and manufactured an interim prototype, which was assembled in the garage of one of the union members. It sought to solve the problem of adapting a manual keyboard to electrical power, and it aroused great interest. Yet interest was not enough when state policies had been reversed, and the new Secretary for Industry was clearly not in the business of democratic industrial innovation. The occupation was called off.

However, if large-scale rescue operations were ruled out, smaller experiments became more possible, as a result of changes in the Department of Employment, which came under the Secretaryship of Albert Booth, a partisan of workers' control ideas who had previously reacted to the UCS work-in by discussing the development of participative forms of nationalisation with the shipbuilders in his own constituency. Funds became available under the Job Creation Programme to help small-scale co-ops. A typical example was reported by Harold Frayman, in *Labour Weekly*.

> "Around lunchtime today a delivery truck will arrive in a Grantham side street, dwarfing the Old Bakery where it stops. A couple of dozen workers, including the entire managerial staff, will bring out hundreds of dresses and skirts loaded on hangers.
>
> There are no miserable faces among the workers. Grantham Workers' Co-operative has completed its fifth full week in production.
>
> 'That's the thing about co-ops', says Ann Griffiths. 'We all have our own jobs — I'm a presser — but we lend a hand where it's needed'. For Celia Wadey — by common consent the driving force behind the idea of a co-op — her best moment in their short history came as she left one woman to work on after everybody else had left. 'Of course I'll be all right'', the woman told her. 'If anyone comes I'll fight to defend this place. After all, part of it belongs to me'.
>
> The enthusiasm at Grantham Fashions is almost missionary. 'If anyone came to us saying they were thinking of setting up a co-op I would tell them to get on with it', says Geoffrey Fincham, cutter, designer and one of the three men on the co-op's 27-strong workforce.
>
> 'I only wish there were more help available to people who wanted to do it', he said.
>
> The co-op knows just how important to get help and just how disheartening it can be to have to overcome what seem like needless obstacles. But now, with a grant from the Job Creation Programme, the co-op's future is guaranteed for at least a year. The members were among 180 workers made redundant when the town's Courtaulds clothing factory announced its closure in autumn 1976. They spent the best part of a year on the dole, while trying to raise money to get the co-op on its feet. On top of the usual fund-raising one of the best things to happen to them was the Silver Jubilee — Celia Wadey and Geoff Fincham spent a week stitching up bunting and raised an extra £100.

A REBIRTH OF CO-OPERATION?

The prospect of lasting jobs after a year of mixed hope and misery is one they are anxious to share, so they are shocked to discover the Job Creation Programme may not help co-ops get going in the future.

Many of their old colleagues are still on the dole or have simply given up working altogether. But Ms Wadey, then National Union of Knitwear and Hosiery Workers shop steward, had no intention of losing the skills accumulated at the old factory.

'One night I was talking to a Labour councillor and said I didn't know much about co-ops, but perhaps we should set one up', she says."[12]

At this point she was advised to contact the Institute for Workers' Control, which she did that same evening.

"The next day Ken Fleet of the IWC talked to us and persuaded us it would work. Without their help I doubt if we could have managed.

Ms Wadey started lobbying her fellow workers. 'Some of them thought I was mad, but about 35 seemed to take to the idea'. In the following months some of the original workers dropped out, but those who remain are now firmly wedded to the idea.

They range from the Co-op employee and Co-operative Party member who explained she wanted to join 'because for me it's a principled thing', to the woman who wasn't quite sure whether South Kesteven, the district council, was Tory or Labour (it's Tory). All of them are confident their venture will succeed.

They are none of them taking home fortunes but in semi-rural Grantham their £40 for a 40 hour week is better than it sounds. They have fixed their wages for at least a year.

Their time clock, like the sewing machines, was donated by Courtaulds — and the JCP grant is conditional on detailed time sheets.

Three of the workers — the men — are paid over the odds. But manager Mike Parnell insists it's not male chauvinism: 'It hadn't even struck me before'.

When Courtaulds closed the factory he was kept on in his job as an accountant, but soon quit to join the co-op.

His job is administration, coping with the forms and finance, and seeking the orders which keep them going. A committee of eight who meet once a week make recommendations on managerial decisions to the monthly staff meetings. Sometimes the general meetings accept the advice and sometimes they don't. But because everyone plays a part there is no argument when decisions have been made, said Geoff Fincham.

Grantham Fashions has had plenty of help. The Institute for Workers' Control, the Industrial Common Ownership Movement and co-op expert Professor John Beishon of the Open University have all given advice and encouragement. Their union has helped them get orders and several unions have sent cash.

Perhaps less predictably, both the local manager of Barclays Bank and Council officers have provided crucial help.

The Manpower Services Commission, responsible to the Government for the Job Creation Programme, is viewed in more ambiguous light. The commission is paying the £100,000 which guarantees the co-op for a year."

It was during 1976 also that the Industrial Common Ownership Act was approved, on the initiative of David Watkins, to provide a legal framework for common ownership and fund the Industrial Common Ownership Movement to the tune of £20,000 per annum. The outcome was remarkable. The number of enterprises registered under Common Ownership rules went from one in 1976 to 27 the following year, 73 in 1978, 134 in 1979 and 224 in 1980.

> "In the first three months of 1980, 32 new industrial co-operatives commenced trading; builders, electronic manufacturers, language schools, printers and publishers, bespoke tailors, newspapers, even a theatre company and a group practice of psychotherapists. Small businesses for the most part but businesses run by people that not only want to earn a living, but to participate fully in the management of their joint enterprise."

As Mike Campbell reports:

> "The new co-operators tend to have explicit social objectives as well as a desire to control their own lives. The people working in the Thames Building Co-operative believe:
>
>> 'That all people should, through their daily lives have the right to work creatively, using their skills to enhance the quality of their work, as well as the quality of their working lives, whilst at the same time they have a duty to ensure that they do nothing which might prevent their fellow workers from achieving the same.'
>
> The people involved in Computercraft say:
>
>> 'We, the founding members of Computercraft Limited, have come together to work co-operatively as a way to produce the software of our choice under the conditions of our choice.
>>
>> We have all been employed in the computer industry before and we wish now to ensure that the product of our work is not used to make people redundant or to control or restrict or kill them. The same techniques have other uses and we would rather explore these.'
>
> The members of the B.B. Abrasives tell us that they are:
>
>> 'A distributive co-operative servicing industry at fair prices, to combat

the ravages of inflation and the assisting of small, medium and other companies to purchase the goods we sell competitively thus helping to cut their overheads, and to give service and advice to the best of our technical ability' "[13]

Of course, hundreds of little enterprises may well seem to be "safe" concessions to industrial democracy. Indeed, there are now fashionable voices to be heard praising them. It is easier to enable new beginnings at a microscopic level than it is to tackle the problems of collapse in old declining basic industries, or to confront the transnational corporations as they lay waste whole communities in the search for a quicker turnover. And yet, had there been no upheaval at UCS, even these modest developments would never have been thinkable. At the same time, the earth-movements which provoked the work-in and sit-in movement will continue to shake the British political economy, and will not fail to renew their challenge to the directors of its most powerful centres.

Footnotes

1. This view was certainly expressed in the Liverpool debates about the occupation of GEC, two years before UCS.
2. See Geoffrey Sheridan's interview with Susan Shapiro: *The Guardian*, 15.6.1972.
3. Worse, NUFLAT Norwich branch officers were "banned from the factory" because they insisted that "the women should abandon their struggle" (*Morning Star* 30 March 1972). According to the *Guardian* (7 April 1972) NUFLAT "put them out of benefit, refused to give them money from a shop floor collection, and asked the local Trades Council not to give them financial support".
4. *Inside Story:* 'How Red was Briant Colour?' No.10, August 1973.
5. See Bel Mooney: The Lessons of Leadgate. *New Statesman*, 27 April 1973.
6. Coates (ed.) *The New Worker Co-operatives*, Spokesman, 1976.
7. Tom Clarke, *Sit-in at Fisher-Bendix,* IWC Pamphlet No.42, 1974.
8. See *The New Worker Co-operatives* and also, for a different view, Ron Mckay and Brian Barr: *The Story of the Scottish Daily News*, Canongate, 1976.
9. For an analysis of the wider meanings of that policy shift see Coates (ed.) *What Went Wrong*, Spokesman, 1979.
10. *Why Imperial typewriters Must Not Close*, IWC Pamphlet No.46, pp.4-5.
11. *Ibid.*, pp.12-13.
12. Reprinted in *Workers' Control Bulletin*, IWC, 1978, No.2, p.13.
13. *Workers' Control*, IWC, 1980, No.4, p.23.

Chapter X

A Conclusion and a New Beginning

By 1975, although it was showing no signs of abating, the uprush of factory occupations had already established its main practical lessons. At a time when new investment meant displacement of labour on a significant scale, struggles about redundancy were bound to become more prevalent and intractable. That the processes of technological unemployment were to be joined by a structural crisis of British industry, as the weakest and least viable competitor in the advanced capitalist world began visibly to flag, lagging further and further behind in a murderously punishing race, only implied that such struggles would be less and less avoidable.

The first slogans of the UCS occupiers came from old socialist text-books. "Nationalise", cried almost everyone. Nationalisation was by no means an inappropriate response, and indeed it will almost certainly continue to be widely applied in further response to developing crisis. But nationalisation, to put matters mildly, is by no means a job-saving expedient. The main nationalised industries in post-war Britain have all been arch-rationalisers. Mining production, to take a typical example, has been maintained with a rapidly dwindling labour force, so that a one-time dominant miners' union has long been relegated to the TUC's middle league, its membership having shrunk well below half its post-war expectations, (and all too likely to shrink yet more when modern collieries come into full production at Selby or the Vale of Belvoir: from whence thousands more jobs will then be wasted away in the older coalfields[1]). The streamlining of railways, fierce labour economies in electricity generating, the transformation of gas supply: all these examples of concentration of production with an ever smaller workforce are too well-known to need rehearsing in detail. The more recent sacrifice of the Steel Industry merely underlines the trend. If any were to doubt such evidence, they need only look to British Leyland: as Michael Barratt Brown has argued, the combined effect of all these labour economies "has at least equalled the job-destruction of the giant transnational companies in closing their plants in Britain".[2] Necessary though an extension of conventional forms of public ownership may be, it will surely not provide all the conditions for the recreation of full employment.

As the slump began at first to take hold of the British economy, more and more workers began to look for militant means of defending their jobs, and sit-ins became widespread. This trend has continued even into the acutely adverse times of the Thatcher administration, while more conventional defensive industrial reactions such as strikes or go-slows were becoming extremely difficult to carry through.

In the second half of 1980, when unemployment rose substantially over 2,000,000, the number of work stoppages declined rapidly:

	Number of strikes beginning in month	
	1979	*1980*
July	185	67
August	218	63
September	172	98
October	196	99
November	131	53
December	53	n.a.

	workers involved in strikes in progress in month	
	1979	*1980*
July	662,000	168,000
August	4,103,000	118,000
September	11,716,000	206,000
October	3,508,000	191,000

A CONCLUSION AND A NEW BEGINNING

| November | 606,000 | 157,000 |
| December | 190,000 | n.a. |

Source: *Employment Gazette*, December 1980.

But even during this economic blizzard, the mere threat of plant occupations could still sometimes serve to improve offers of compensation for loss of jobs, since managements often wished to avoid the long exposure to critical commentary which, it has been learnt, very commonly accompanies sit-ins or work-ins.

As far as job-protection is concerned, the range of possible demands which could be made by workers was much enriched by the early success of the first handful of producer co-operatives. Here was a form of common ownership which could be carried through on a small scale, which gave the initiative to workpeople themselves, and which did not depend on centralised bureaucratic forms of management. For the micro-sector of the economy this was an option which was bound to prove attractive. Even so, critics were not slow to point out that the new co-ops emerging from work-ins often employed fewer people than had been originally dismissed, while those re-employed commonly accepted modified work practices, which would have been resisted if they had been introduced by a private boss. Often such critics were blind to the similar, but more pronounced, failings of nationalised concerns. Of course, people are willing to pay a price for self-management, once they come to believe it possible. Yet for the collapsing large firms, for derelict old industries, for multinational subsidiaries, such prescriptions have been very difficult to apply, and it is not surprising that they have seldom taken practical effect. That co-operation will grow can hardly be doubted. As unemployment soars towards the three-million level, the task of re-employing so vast an army falls well outside the reach of normal central government initiative. Large manufacturing projects are in any case prone to be capital intensive, so that new jobs each cost a prodigious investment. More: such projects take time to plan and launch, and it is indeed quite common for them to involve a longer span between the drawing board and the first deliveries of actual products than the entire lifetime of a British Parliament. Bureaucratically initiated plans which require from five to seven years in which to bear fruit, while they will be very much needed, will not be enough for any Government which seeks the early restoration of full employment.[3]

Of course, public services, especially the personal social services, are commonly labour intensive, and they can absorb a large labour force if only they can be adequately funded. But the continuous displacement of workers by innovative technology in manufacturing industry will ensure that there are strenuous demands for more co-operative and municipal enterprise, as well as for the revival of such welfare services as pre-school education and a functioning health service. Decentralised initiatives will become as important in this process as central state policies, and this may mean innovations which go far beyond the early example of the sit-in movement.

Such stratagems may well come easily to a trade union movement which has been to school with UCS and its responding imitators. There has been a further stimulus to learning in the related experience of the Lucas Aerospace workers, whose combine committee prepared a thousand-page blueprint for conversion to socially useful production when their company was facing the possibility of serious contraction during that brief interlude when it seemed that military spending might be seriously cut back.[4] The Lucas stewards researched areas of potential need in a wide variety of health and social service pressure groups, and also called upon rich resources of inventiveness among the members they represented. Their alternative corporate plan, which has been described in some considerable detail elsewhere, included market-oriented proposals for innovative high-technology projects such as the "power-pack", a device which couples a small internal combustion engine to a stack of batteries in order to provide almost silent motive power at savings of 50% in fuel consumption and 80% in pollution; or for greatly improved heat pumps and advanced wind-generators. It also included a variety of products which might normally be aimed at the caring services, such as kidney machines, which were already manufactured in inadequate numbers by enterprises within the Lucas Group. Mike Cooley, a spokesman of the Lucas Committee, provides a moving report of one of the inventions which the Lucas workpeople pioneered:

> "Before we even started the corporate plan our members at the Wolverhampton plant visited a centre for children with Spina Bifida and were horrified to see that the only way they could propel themselves about was literally by crawling on the floor. So they designed a vehicle which subsequently became known as Hobcart — it was highly successful and the Spina Bifida Association of Australia wanted to order 2,000 of these. Lucas would not agree to manufacture these because they said it was incompatible with their product range and at that time the corporate plan was not developed and we were not able to press for this. But the design and development of this product were significant in another sense: Mike Parry Evans, its designer, said that it was one of the most enriching experiences of his life when he actually took the Hobcart down and saw the pleasure on the child's face — it meant more to him, he said, than all the design activity he had been involved in up to then. For the first time in his career *he actually saw the person who was going to use the product that he had designed.* It was enriching also in another sense because he was intimately in contact with a social human problem. He literally had to make a clay mould of the child's back so that the seat would support it properly. It was also fulfilling in that for the first time he was working in the multi-disciplinary team together with a medical type doctor, a physiotherapist and a health visitor. I mention this because it illustrates very graphically that it is untrue to suggest that aerospace technologies are only interested in complex esoteric technical problems. It can be far more enriching for them if they are allowed to relate their technology to really human and social problems."[5]

There were other numerous creative designs. One was that of the road-rail vehicle, which can drive on rails where these exist, but retract its flanges in order to navigate roads when it reaches them. This vehicle would cut the expenditure involved in developing new railways by a considerable factor, since it would not be necessary to tunnel or drive costly cuttings, because the vehicle could navigate inclines as steep as one in six on its pneumatic tyres. (Conventional railways only function with inclines of not more than 1:80, which means that even before oil-inflation they commonly cost £1 million per track mile.)

The Lucas initiative was originally provoked in a meeting which took place between the shop stewards and Tony Benn whilst he was still Industry Minister. Nonetheless, it encountered sustained passive resistance by the Wilson Government after the 1975 U-turn.[6] Although the Labour Party, as distinct from the Government, enthusiastically embraced the alternative plan, Government intervention to bring it into force was never forthcoming. The new device of planning agreements was simply not activated, and it was left to others to support this quite extraordinary movement. By the 1980s, the more adventurous local authorities were beginning to be urgently interested in rational projects for job creation, and the search began for forms of local enterprise which could draw upon the Lucas experience.

It is safe to say that events like these have changed the intellectual map of the Labour Movement.

As the issues raised go home in their full force, we begin to see the possibilities for a socialism based upon local initiative, creating new forms of productive association and establishing a new relationship between social planning for community needs and the operation of a changed market. The mental barriers to this development have begun to go down, one after another.

Among the fences which have sagged, sometimes to the point of collapse, has been the once formidable barrier of property as an institution. Property has always been a relationship between people, not, as it has often seemed, a relationship of people to things. But commonly people have seen it upside down, as Marx insisted in the first chapter of *Capital*. He was not the sole originator of this insight. "The first person", said Rousseau, "who, having fenced off a plot of ground, took it into his head to say *this is mine* and found people simple enough to believe him, was the true founder of civil society". That is to say, property consists in thinking of a claim, and persuading one's neighbours to accept it. Once the idea has currency, we are in "civil society".

The right to property as exclusive private use had hitherto been justified by different philosophers, either as a right to that with which one's labour had been mixed (the view associated with John Locke) or as an act to ensure the public peace (as Hobbes saw it). Hobbes presumed that before the establishment of the "sovereign power" all men were equally entitled to all existing natural objects, "which necessarily causeth war", so that private property was both "necessary to peace" and dependent on sovereign power for its enforcement, and therefore existence.

For Hegel, who identified the State as the embodiment of Reason, and who saw freedom as existing only within the framework of its laws, this judgement could be simplified into the catchphrase "property is the first reality of freedom". For Locke, every man "has a property in his own person. This nobody has any right to but himself. The Labour of his body, and the work of his hands, we may properly say, are his. Whatsoever, then, he removes out of the state that Nature hath provided and left it in, he hath mixed his labour with it, and joined it to something that is his own, and thereby makes it his property".

Doctrines such as these all had powerful liberal implications, (albeit different ones) when small producers were the predominant economic force. But they came, however, to have a radically different meaning as production and ownership were concentrated into ever fewer controlling hands. Marx witnessed this in his youth, when he saw the Prussian Diet busily abolishing the common rights of the peasantry. If property *could* be monopolised, then it *would* be monopolised, he concluded. Liberal philosophers drew similar conclusions more timidly, as when T.H. Green insisted that property had "become incompatible with its idea" when it began to present an obstacle to free development of the personality rather than a stimulus to such development. If one's freedom to develop one's faculties depends on access to property, and if the prior concentration of ownership prevents such access, then property is now the basis of unfreedom, whatever the philosophers thought before. Over the centuries we have seen an evolution from little watermills with a few dozen employees to transnational companies with greater resources than entire nation states. "Monopoly" in this sense has become a salient fact of life. Yet attitudes to property have, for a long time, been mixed. Old doctrines have held their force long after they have ceased to be true in any but the most marginal sense. Of course people will defend private property in the marrows or beans grown on their allotments by the persistent application of their own muck and sweat. But this response will not offer them any guarantee of freedom when their interests as employees or citizens run foul of General Motors or the General Electric Company.

A famous survey by Colin Hurry and Associates, in 1959,[7] showed a small but significant majority of Labour voters in 129 marginal constituencies were opposed to any further nationalisation. Labour voters divided 36% to 42% on the issue. The survey was crudely designed and rightly provoked strong criticism at the time: but the adverse vote on nationalisation could not be explained by the huge rationalisation programmes which were subsequently to hit these industries, in the following decade. The result could in part, perhaps, be accounted for because nationalisation was not responsible for any perceptible change in the status and participatory powers of the workers who were directly affected by it: but this would undoubtedly have been a minority judgement, since those wanting greater democratic control would normally seek reform of existing nationalised industries, which was quite compatible with an extension of nationalisation, and, indeed, likely to provoke one. No, there are strong grounds for believing that this kind of reaction represented genuine opposition, which in that time reflected deeply ingrained received attitudes to property.

Such thinking certainly affected the argument in the Labour and trade union movements, and was involved in the background of the debate on the revision of the Labour Party's constitution, in which attempts were made by Hugh Gaitskell and his associates to amend Clause IV, suppressing the Party's commitment to the "common ownership of the means of production, distribution and exchange". At the grass roots, one commonly heard arguments in favour of private property which harked back to classical liberal theory. "How would you like it" one could be asked "if you worked all your life to build up a shop, and the Government came and took it?" Such property rested on the fact that its owner had "mixed his (or her) labour" with the equipment at issue, and it would easily have been understood by Locke two and a half centuries earlier. It had, however, nothing whatever to do with owning ICI or Rolls Royce, which aggregates combined far more labour than had ever been mixed with anything by their founding fathers, or indeed their succeeding stockholders. Why was it possible to apply it, erroneously, to such different cases? This has been explained, sociologically, by the concept of reference groups. People commonly identify with others like themselves. They compare themselves with their peers, and not with outlandish outsiders. Only some great crisis or trauma will provoke a realistic focus on the implications of outsider behaviour. Normally, next door, or the next workplace, give us our standards of expectation.

When a group of adult students interviewed poor people in a Nottingham slum, they found that many of them defined "wealth" as a weekly income which was actually below national average earnings, and few thought of it as implying ownership of any assets at all. Those few saw wealth as being "a house and a car". Half a million shares in Boots or Players was a thought not only completely outside their daily experience, but beyond any practical imagination.[8]

The "revisionist" current in the Labour Party were, of course, greatly more sophisticated than this. In *Twentieth Century Socialism*, a classic statement of the arguments of the right-wing grouping, we find three key propositions supporting the view that "the case for complete common ownership" was misconceived.

> "Once the state owns all capital resources, no one but the state is able to take decisions as to their disposal. Every business activity is subservient to the will of the government. There is no freedom to experiment with ideas which have not won state approval. The man who wishes to risk or dare is a misfit — or worse. To eliminate all private cpaital is to open the road to totalitarianism.
>
> The second misconception lay in the belief that ownership was only dangerous in private hands. Once it had been transferred to public hands — so it was thought — the power it represented would be relatively harmless, for society would control it for social ends. Experience has now shown that the power of ownership, even in public hands, may still be dangerous. It is still open to abuse and the individual has still to struggle to assert his rights in face of it. Ways have to be found to control the powers of ownership, whether they are privately or publicly held.
>
> The third, and perhaps most serious, misconception was the belief that ownership was one indivisible right, which could be held only as a whole — either by private persons or by public authorities; an industry was either wholly in private or in public control. In fact ownership consists of a bundle of rights. These rights are not sacred; they are upheld by the state and society. They are not fixed and unalterable; they can be changed and modified to any degree that state and society desires, and indeed they are constantly changing. Nor are they indivisible. Each separate right can be limited separately and by different methods; some can be in private and some in public hands.
>
> Take, for example, the main rights associated with the ownership of business enterprise. There is the right to decide what is to be produced, the right to retain profits for personal use, the right

to dispose of capital assets, the right to hire and fire. None of these rights are now absolute; each may be limited in one way or another. What is produced may be subject to direct government control, or, alternatively, to controls over the equipment or materials which the industry may use. Distributed profits may be curtailed by taxation, or by legislation to limit dividends. Capital transactions may be regulated. The engagement and dismissal of workers may be made to obey conditions agreed with the trade unions. Each right of ownership may in turn be circumscribed or transferred; indeed the rights of ownership can be invaded to such an extent that ownership no longer confers power. Little but the title — and the right to dispose of it — remains.

The twentieth century has witnessed how, step by step, the old unrestricted rights of ownership in regard to labour have been whittled away — through legislation, through trade union organisation, through full employment — with the result that the power relationship between capital and labour today stands transformed even when ownership is still in private hands".[9]

Arguing only on the plane of the authors of this passage, it is easy to see that they in turn share three misconceptions. They conceive of common ownership as purely state ownership, and the ownership of a unitary state at that. But common ownership includes local, municipal, co-operative and syndicalist possibilities, as well as central state ones. It also includes the possibility of "arms length" relations with the state, such as those enjoyed by universities, or the BBC, or "responsible bodies" in adult education, which enjoy Government funding, but remain autonomous and self-governing, subject only to certain principles of accountability. There is no a priori reason why crudely centralised state ownership must predominate in a common ownership economy.

Secondly, while they are quite right to stress the need to defend individual rights against state institutions, they do not appreciate the potential of democratic control mechanisms to do precisely this, and they miss this crucial arm of socialist strategy because they identify public ownership with rigid, hierarchic public corporations of the type we have inherited from Herbert Morrison, much to our cost and woe.

Thirdly, while they are also right to stress that the bundle of actual rights involved in private ownership is subject to erosion, not only by planning statutes, but also by collective bargaining, they do not appreciate the powerful pressure to concentration, which crystallises great private agglomerates with ample powers to sidestep or even manipulate legislation. If taxation can curtail profits, transfer pricing by multinationals can avoid taxation. We have, since the 1950s, obtained ample evidence of how strictly limited and one-sided is the perception of this foolishly unguarded and optimistic analysis.[10]

And a rich part of this evidence came home to the trade union movement during the work-ins and sit-ins. We need only listen to Jack Spriggs, uncovering the manipulations of the Fisher-Bendix management, to put an entirely different valency on changes in the content of property rights to that proposed as appropriate by the Labour revisionists. Indeed, public involvement in the funding of privately controlled enterprise had actually augmented unaccountable power, rather than restraining it.

When the workers at Plessey's began their action, it was in protest at the abuse of former public property by a private concern. At one sit-in after another, millions of public money were inextricably involved in the equation the workers had to unravel. Throughout industry, for several years previously, all new investment had attracted a minimum public subsidy of 20%. Social democracy had reduced itself to a policy of generous public handouts to private interests, without any public control. Creeping state intervention, by the time of the '70s, had thus made a complete muddle of the frontier between private and public zones of investment, without the slightest degree of public sharing in actual responsibility or power. Even the phenomenal growth of employee pension funds, which resulted from successful legislative intervention and collective bargaining during the years of full employment, had not substantially increased workpeople's collective power. Control of vast funds of employee savings in the most part eluded their "owners", and decisions on investment were predominantly the prerogative of the corporate rich. Yet the fact remained that large sums of money which were deployed by pension funds and insurance companies were the property of industrially voteless working people. The old property shibboleths, once one had to examine them, became quite insupportable.

More: glued up as property had become, it was quite "incompatible with its idea" if that idea had anything to do with self-fulfilment for the legions of ordinary wage-slaves. After two decades of consensus in politics, in which "the main rights associated with the ownership of business enterprise" had been fixed more or less constantly at the point already determined at the time of the *Socialist Union* manifesto,[11] no real transfer of power had thereby ensued. Modest concessions to rights in employment had been legislated, first in redundancy payment provisions, and later in the development of tribunal law. But the first of these in no way enhanced the social power of workpeople in their organisations, while it was specifically designed to increase labour mobility, or the availability of labour power as a resource to be used by capital. In other words, it allowed for personal cash benefits in order the better to uphold collective subordination. The second achieved its main extension as a result of the Heath Government's Industrial Relations Act of 1971, and while it conferred certain (largely inadvertent) benefits on labour, it was accompanied by many other deeply resented curbs on purely defensive trade union powers. The rights vested in ownership have not been absolute, that is true: but they never were. But they do still confer substantial arbitrary power, which was clearly exposed in the succession of crises which provoked one factory occupation after another. It is one thing for Town and Country Planning laws to control random advertising: this is a circumscription of ownership rights, but it, and half a hundred similar limitations, bear not at all on the strategic powers "to decide what is produced, . . . to retain profits . . . to dispose of capital assets . . . to hire and fire". On the contrary, some sit-ins took place to prevent naked cases of asset stripping, or to insist that social property remain social property, or very commonly to assert elementary claims which were in no way otherwise guaranteed in the early 'seventies, all the "revisionist" tracts of the previous quarter century notwithstanding. Not one of the participants in these actions could accept that "Little but the title — and the right to dispose of it — remains". Had such a roseate view been true, their often bitter ordeals of struggle would have been quite unnecessary.

As loyal workmen and women suddenly confronted factory closures, they also confronted the hollowness of the claim that "the power relationship between labour and capital today stands transformed". Experience had pronounced a sombre verdict on all such nostrums, and that experience was responsible for the gathering shift of opinion within the Labour Movement, which is still in motion.

On the shoulders of those who fought the battles of UCS, Plesseys and KME, a distinguished political philosopher has propounded an interesting new view of property, which opens important perspectives.

> "Property", he tells us "although it must always be an individual right, need not be confined, as liberal theory has confined it, to a right to exclude others from the use or benefit of some thing, but may equally be an individual right not to be excluded by others from the use or benefit of some thing. When property is so understood, the problem of liberal-democratic theory is no longer a problem of putting limits on the property right, but of supplementing the individual right to exclude others by the individual right not to be excluded by others. The latter right may be held to be the one that is most required by the liberal-democratic ethic, and most implied in a liberal concept of the human essence. The right not to be excluded by others may provisionally be stated as the individual right to equal access to the means of labour and/or the means of life."[12]

A CONCLUSION AND A NEW BEGINNING

This thought, which we owe to C.B. Macpherson, does not in itself solve practical political problems, any more than Locke could posthumously administer the American Union after it had enshrined his outlook in its constitution. But it does open a door to a whole area of political argument, in which the workers of Glasgow, or Liverpool, or London, will doubtless become engaged. In an important sense, they already have. By asserting their right to work, to "access to the means of labour", these men and women were not appealing for totalitarian controls, censorship, political psychiatry or suppression of personal liberty. All of them rightly took for granted all the established liberal freedoms of speech, assembly, worship, and the press. They were not seeking full-time employment in a Polish state with government-controlled trade unions. If they had any criticisms of democratic institutions, those criticisms would emphasise the need for fuller, not less stringent, accountability and openness.

But they did show, both in their many brilliant individual initiatives and in their courageous joint activities, a burning need for quite new institutions, from which none could be excluded from the means to the fullest moral life available to any. The rebirth of socialism, which is what we are talking about, will be a true renaissance of individual human freedom, if it takes its growth-points from such people as these. Precisely inasmuch as shipbuilders, coal-miners, clerks and engineers are determined to widen the real areas of choice and the material scope for self-fulfilment which are available in their own personal lives, and inasmuch as their combined actions serve these individual goals, the new commonwealth itself begins to come to life.

In Britain, in 1981, three million people will soon be without work. Enterprise is a word which now means inertia and greed. Authority is a widely used synonym for unreasonableness. But private property once meant that "town air was free air", because the guildsman's scissors or hammers were the basis of his independent livelihood. Now it means transnational companies and wholesale displacement of labour. Words change when people change, and we can join our forces to create a vocabulary in which enterprise becomes in truth a shared effort to improvement and mutual care, and authority is understood as uncoerced admiration for example, and nothing more.

Generations of our forebears, in times when windmills were thought to be sophisticated inventions, could imagine a world in which each might grow in the love, care, and effort of others, and all might take uninhibited delight in the achievements of each. Such Utopian thoughts have been unfashionable in an age of lasers, micro-chips and revisionism. But they are stirring again, and however troublesome they may be to mediamen and entrepreneurs, the sense they make will become apparent to millions of good people, as they in their turns face the issues which provoked this little book and its innumerable inspirers.

Footnotes

1. For a discussion of the data on these issues, see Ken Coates: *Ashfield: What Went Wrong?* IWC Pamphlet No.53, 1978 and *Industrial Development and Democratic Planning — The Case of Belvoir*, IWC Pamphlet No.61, 1978.
2. Michael Barratt Brown: *Unemployment and Economic Theory* in *Workers' Control*, No.3, 1981.
3. Already in 1981 many local Labour Parties have begun work on proposals for local enterprise boards to stimulate co-operative and direct municipal production. The London Labour Party is proposing to devote the proceeds of a two penny rate (£40m) to this kind of work. The Sheffield Labour-controlled council has set up a working party with local trade unionists to examine employment-creating possibilities. Various local government groupings have examined the possibility of introducing legislation (as is their right under existing law) to extend their powers in this field.
4. See Ken Coates (editor) *The Right to Useful Work*, Spokesman, 1978, Chapters VIII, IX. Also *Turning Industrial Decline into Expansion*, Interim Report prepared by Lucas Aerospace Confederation Trade Union Committee, February 1979.
5. *The Right to Useful Work*, p.201-2.
6. *Democracy versus the Circumlocution Office* by the Lucas Aerospace Combine Shop Stewards' Committee, IWC Pamphlet No.65, 1979.

A CONCLUSION AND A NEW BEGINNING

7. *Survey of Public Opinion on Nationalisation*, Colin Hurry and Associates, London, September 1959, p.4 et seq.
8. Ken Coates and Richard Silburn: *Poverty, The Forgotten Englishmen*, Penguin, 1981, Chapter 7, also *Beyond the Bulldozer*, Nottingham University, Department of Adult Education, 1980, pp.101-15.
9. Socialist Union (Allan Flanders and Rita Hinden) *Twentieth Century Socialism*, Penguin Books, 1956, pp.125-7.
10. This is lucidly presented by Stuart Holland in *The Socialist Challenge*, Quartet 1975.
11. *Twentieth Century Socialism,* op.cit.
12. C.B. Macpherson: *Property*, Blackwell, 1978, p.201.

Bibliography

The student of this topic suffers from the fact that the most necessary references are to articles in the press, including parts of the press which are shifting and ephemeral, and seldom filed in public libraries. Among the recurrent sources, the following daily journals are the most prominent: *The Financial Times, The Guardian, The Morning Star, The Times*. The weekly newspapers which contain regular reports include *Labour Weekly, Red Weekly, The Socialist Worker, Tribune* and the *Sunday Times*. Among less frequent journals, *Labour Research* and *Workers' Control*, the Bulletin of the IWC, contain much information.

Books and Pamphlets

Balfour, Campbell: *Participation in Industry*, Croom Helm, 1974.
Balfour, Campbell (Ed): *Workers' Co-operatives: A Vital Experiment in Participation in Industry*, Croom Helm, 1973.
Barratt Brown, Michael: *From Labourism to Socialism*, Spokesman, 1973.
Barratt Brown, Michael: *UCS — The Social Audit*, IWC Pamphlet No.26.
Barratt Brown, Michael and Coates, Ken: *The Trade Union Register 3, Spokesman, 1973*.
Benello, C. George and Roussopolos, D: *The Case for Participatory Democracy*, Grossman, NY 1971.
Benn, Tony: *Speeches by Tony Benn*, Spokesman, 1974.
Blumberg, Paul: *Industrial Democracy*, Constable, 1968.
Buchan, Alasdair: *The Right to Work*, Calder and Boyars, 1972.
Coates, Ken: *Can the Workers Run Industry?* Spokesman, 1968.
Coates, Ken: *Essays on Industrial Democracy*, Spokesman, 1971.
Coates, Ken: *Industrial Democracy and Democratic Planning: The Case of Belvoir*, IWC Pamphlet No.61.
Coates, Ken (Ed): *The Right to Useful Work*, Spokesman, 1978.
Coates, Ken (Ed.): *The New Worker Co-operatives*, Spokesman, 1976.
Coates, Ken (Ed.): *What Went Wrong*, Spokesman, 1979.
Coates, Ken & Topham, Tony: *Catching up with the Times: How the TUC got the message about Workers' Control*, IWC, 1974.
Coates, Ken & Topham, Tony: *Industrial Democracy in Great Britain*, Three Volumes, Spokesman, 1975.
Coates, Ken & Topham, Tony: *Trade Unions in Britain*, Spokesman, 1980.

Clarke, Tom: *Sit-in at Fisher Bendix,* IWC Pamphlet No.42.
Derrick, Paul and Phipps, J.F: *Co-ownership, Co-operation and Control,* Longmans, 1969.
Eaton, John, Hughes, John & Coates, Ken: *UCS,* IWC Pamphlet No.25.
Fleet, Ken: *Whatever Happened at UCS?,* IWC Pamphlet No.28.
Greenwood, J: *Worker Sit-ins and Job Protection,* Gower Press, 1977.
Hart, Finlay & Thompson, W: *The UCS Work-in,* Lawrence & Wishart, 1972.
Herron, Frank: *Labour Market in Crisis,* Macmillan, 1975.
Holland, Stuart: *Strategy for Socialism,* Spokesman, 1975.
Holland, Stuart: *The Socialist Challenge,* Quartet Books, 1975.
Hunnius, Gerry, et al: *Workers' Control,* Random House, 1973.
Johns, Stephen: *Reformism on the Clyde,* Socialist Labour League, 1973.
Johnson, Ernie: *Industrial Action,* Arrow Books, 1975.
Levinson, Charles: *Industry's Democratic Revolution,* Allen & Unwin, 1974.
Linder, Walter: *The Great Flint Sit-down Strike against GM,* Solidarity, 1969.
MacPherson, C.B: *Property,* Blackwell, 1978.
Maire, Edmond & Piaget, Charles: *Lip '73,* Combats Seuil, 1973.
McGill, Jack: *Crisis on the Clyde,* Davis-Poynter, 1973.
McKay, Ron & Barr, Brian: *The Story of the Scottish Daily News,* Canongate, 1976.
Metra Consulting Group: *An Analysis of Sit-ins,* London, 1972.
Metra Consulting Group: *The Worker Sit-in in Britain,* Oxford, 1975.
Miller, Sir Bernard: *Ernest Bader Memorial Lecture 1975, Scott Bader Commonwealth, 1975.*
Murray, Alex: UCS; The Fight for the Right to Useful Work, CPGB 1971.
Murray, Robin: *The Anatomy of Bankruptcy,* Spokesman, 1972.
Nicholson, Brian: *UCS — An Open Letter,* IWC Pamphlet No.27.
North-East TU Studies Unit: *Workers' Occupations and the North-East Experience,* 1976.
Potter, Beatrice: *The Co-operative Movement,* Swan Sonnenschein, 1892.
Preis, Art: *Labour's Giant Step,* Pathfinder, 1968.
Roberts, Ernie: *Workers' Control,* Allen & Unwin, 1973.
Slater, Montague: *Stay Down Miner,* Lawrence and Wishart, 1936.
Thompson, W. and Hart, Finlay: *The UCS Work-in,* Lawrence and Wishart, 1972.
TUC: *Annual Report,* 1971-75.
TUC: *Interim Report on Industrial Democracy,* 1973.

BIBLIOGRAPHY

TUC: *Report on Industrial Democracy,* 1974.
Union Action Committee: *Why Imperial Typewriters Must Not Close,* IWC Pamphlet, No.46.
Wilson, Harold: *Three Speeches on Industrial Democracy,* The Labour Party, 1973.

Articles

This list does not include news reports, but only feature articles.

Agenor: 'Signposts to Workers' Control' No.53, August 1975.
Baur, Chris: 'Giving Scotland its News', *Financial Times,* 5.8.74.
Bishop, Terry: 'When the Workers Take Control', *Personnel Management,* March 1973.
Bond, C.E.: 'Under New Management'. A play produced at Liverpool's Everyman Theatre, 1975.
Brind, Donald: 'Triumph for Bike Men', *Labour Weekly,* 2 August 1974.
British & Irish Communist Organisation: 'The Triumph Worker Directors', *The Communist,* April 1974.
Cartwright, Peter & Owen, Geoffrey: 'Meriden — A Dream that may end in a rude awakening', *Financial Times,* 7 March 1975.
Coleman, Barry: 'Will a 1965 model sell in 1975', *The Guardian,* 24 March 1975.
Co-operative Producer Federation Ltd: *The Case for Co-operative Co-Partnership,* Leicester 1973.
Co-operative Producer Federation Ltd: *Co-operative Worker Participation,* Leicester 1973.
Corina, Maurice: 'Old Hands Can Help the New Co-ops', *Times,* 20.3.75.
Crisp, Jason: 'Scottish Good News, a Management Account', *Accountancy Age,* 7.3.75.
Derrick, Paul: 'Are Workers' Co-ops the Answer?', *Platform,* November 1974.
Eccles, Tony: 'Fighting an Underfunded Way', *The Guardian,* 12.3.75.
Fryer, John: 'Co-op or Bust?', *Sunday Times,* 12.1.75.
Fryer, John & Elsworth-Jones, Will: 'Crunch Time for the . . . Workers' Co-ops', *Sunday Times,* 22 December 1973.
Fryer, John: 'Why Benn is on his own', *Sunday Times,* 1.12.74.
GEC-EE Workers' Takeover, IWC, 1969.
Gretton, John: 'To Sit or not to Sit', *New Society,* 15.6.72.
Huckfield, Leslie: 'The Spirit of Meriden', *Tribune,* 9 August 1974.
Inside Story: 'How Red was Briant Colour?', No.10, August 1973.
International Co-operative Alliance: *Industrial Democracy and Social Ownership,* Co-operative Union, 1974.

Jack, Ian et al: 'How Maxwell Sabotaged the Workers' Dream', *Sunday Times*, 21.9.75.
Kelly, Stephen: 'IPD', *Tribune,* 29.11.74.
Labour Weekly: 'Workers' Control: Is this the start of something big?', 2.8.74.
London Co-operative Society: *How to start a Workers' Co-op,* June 1975.
Marks, Malcolm: 'The Battle at Fisher Bendix', *International Socialism,* 1973.
Mills, A: 'Factory Work-ins', *New Society,* 22.8.74.
Mooney, Bel: 'The Lessons of Leadgate', 27.4.73.
Norman, Philip: 'We Eat, Sleep, Ride . . . and Love Motorcycles', *Sunday Times* Colour Supplement, 19 November 1974.
Owen, Nicholas: 'Co-operative with a Conglomerate Output', *Financial Times,* 14.2.75.
Private Eye: 'Hock of the North', 18.4.75.
Red Mole: 'Fisher Bendix Occupied', 24.1.72.
Sawtell, Roger: *How to Change to Common Ownership,* ICOM, London, April 1975.
Scottish News Enterprises Ltd: *Prospectus,* 7.3.75.
Shapiro, Susan: 'Fakenham Report', *The Guardian*, 15.6.72.
Solidarity: *Under New Management?* Pamphlet No.32, 1972.
Sparks, Colin: 'The Co-operative Solution', *International Socialism*, No.73, December 1974.
Taylor, Robert: 'Patriots of Meriden', *New Society*, 8th August 1974.
Whitfield, David: 'Northern Ireland's Workers' Co-ops, *Morning Star*, 22.10.74.
Wyles, John: 'The First Workers' Co-ops', *Financial Times*, 14.2.75.

Index

In this index, while surnames are listed conventionally, company and business names are listed in the alphabetic order of the first part of their normal title, so that, for example, Archibald Edmeston will appear under A. Trades Unions are listed under their normal acronyms, which are decoded in the glossary.

A

ACTT 114
Airlie, Jimmy 30, 32, 34, 39, 107
Alexander, Prof Ken 85
Alexandria 49, 113
Allen, Jim 19
Allis Chalmers 12, 54, 56 et seq, 101, 124
APEX 114
Archibald Edmeston 103
Argyle Works 49
Arkwright, R. 17
ASTMS 80, 102, 114
AUEW 22, 41, 55, 57, 67, 79, 113, 114
AUEW Head Office sit-in 105
Austin Pickergills 25
Australia, work-ins 35

B

Bakers 114
Bamfords 59
Barber, A. 98
Barr, Sammy 21, 22
Barratt Brown, Michael 48, 86, 87 et seq, 150
Barrow Shipyards 42
Bason and Son 104
BB Abrasives 146
Beishon, Prof J. 146
Benn, Tony 21, 22, 25, 29, 33, 70, 84, 138, 140, 154
Big Flame, the 19
Big Hewer, the 19
Bishop, Terry 37, 116
Boggis, Fred 14, 19
Boilermakers 114
Booth, Albert 42, 144
Boots Co. Ltd. 158

BP Chemicals 105
Bradford Co-operative Cabinet Makers 15
Brashaw, Mr 65
Briant Colour Printing 76, 107 et seq, 124, 134
British Leyland 105, 150
British Motor Corporation 62
British Steel Corporation 76, 80, 81, 103
Bromsgrove nailmakers 15
Brotherhood Works, Peterborough 106
BSA Motor Cycles 75, 101
Buchan, Asasdair 37
Bulletin, IWC 116
Bullock Report 140
Burgess, F.H. 57

C

Campbell, Mike 146
Carns, Sidney 65
Carrington-Viyella 106
CAST 68
CAV Fazakerly 105
Chadwick, G. 116
Charles MacNeil 105
Cinema Action 68
Clarke, Tom 147
Clay, Mr 127
Collective contract 137
Combine committees 32, 55, 105, 107
Communications of employers 119
Communist Party 40, 113
Company security 121
Computercraft 146
Conlyon, Fred 136

Conspiracy 219
Constructional Engineers' Union 125
Control by employers 118
Conveyancer Trucks 103
Cooley, Mike 153
Co-operative Bass Dressers 15
Co-operative Bedroom Suite Manufacturers 15
Co-operative Insurance 102
Criminal Law Act 1977 128 et seq
"Criminal Trespass" Bill 127
Courtaulds 144

D

Daily Record 53
DATA 78
Davies, John 11, 21, 26, 77, 96
Davies and Metcalf 103
Derby Turnouts 14
Dockers' Next Step 42
Dooley, Arthur 68
Douglas, Dick 72
Douglas, Ken 25, 84
Dudley nailmakers 15
Dyers and Bleachers 114

E

East Lancs Road Plant, English Electric 29
Eaton Corporation 106
EEC directives 123
EEPTU 79, 114
Emerson, R.W. 17
Employers' countermeasures 116
Engineering Employers' Federation 105
Engineers' Short-time movement 14
Evans, Mike Parry 153
Everyman Theatre 68

F

Fairfields shipyard 24
Fakenham 76, 115, 133, 137
Ferranti 104
Field, Frank 93
Financial Times 54, 60, 70, 71, 72, 73, 81, 111
Fincham, G. 144

Fisher-Bendix 12, 60 et seq, 101, 133, 139, 160
Flanders, A. 165
Fleet, Ken 37, 87
Flexibox, Sharston 103
Follows and Bate 103
Forcible Entry Acts 129
Fords 116
Fords Cologne 120
Fords Dagenham 120
Fords Doncaster 120
Fords Genk 120
Foster-Wheeler 106
'Four Wise Men' 26, 31
Francis Shaw 103
Fraser, Simon 67
Frayman, Harold 144
Fryer, John 71

G

Gainsborough-Cornard's 105, 106
Gaitskell, H.T.N. 157
Gallacher, Alex 53
Gardners 12
Garrard Engineering 107
GEC, Merseyside 27 et seq, 75, 147, 156
GEC switchgear 103
Geddes Committee 24, 88
General Motors 156
Glasgow 9
Glasgow Co-operative Coopers 14
Glasgow Herald 72
GMWU 114
Govan Shipyard 24, 36, 89
Gramsci, Antonio 13
Grand National Consolidated Trade Union 14
Grantham Fashions 144-5
Grantham, Roy 114
Green, Jack 51, 52
Green, T.H. 156
Greening, E.O. 15, 16
Gretten, John 82, 116
Griffiths, Ann 144
Guardian 72, 82, 147
Guest, Keen and Nettlefold 15, 102
Guild Socialists 137

H

Harland and Wolff 88

INDEX

Hart, Finlay 37
Hawker Siddely Aviation 103
Heath, Edward 26, 123, 161
Heffer, Eric 67
Hegel, G.W.F. 125, 154
Henri, Adrian 68
Hepper, A.E. 24, 85
Hinden, Rita 165
Hobbes, T. 154
Hobcart 153
Holland, Stuart 165
Horner, Arthur 18
Hosiery Workers 145
Hoyles, Andrée 18
Hughes, Hugh 58
Hughes, John 91
Hurry, Colin 156

I

ICI 79, 157
Imperial Typewriters 112, 116, 140 et seq
Industrial Common Ownership Movement 146
Industrial injuries 31
Industrial Relations Act 161
Inglis, Hugh 52
Inside Story 81, 116, 147
Institute for Workers' Control 9, 24, 27, 56, 66, 72, 77, 81, 85, 89, 98, 116, 145
International Property Development 71, 139
Ironmonger, Sir Ron 80

J

Jackson, J.A. 125
Jenkins, Clive 114
Job Creation Programme 144
John Brown Shipyard 22, 88
Johns, Stephen 48
Johnston, William 71
Jones Bakers 57
Jones, Jack 40, 113
Joseph Robinson 103

K

Kearns Richards 104
Kearton, Lord 54
Kelly, 'Cashdown' 45

Kent miners 108
Keynes, Lord 98
Kidney machines 153
Kirkby 60 et seq
Kirkby Manufacturing and Engineering 139 et seq, 162
Knowles, G.C.K. 18

L

Labour Party 41, 70, 140, 154
Labour Research 88
Labour Weekly 144
Lancashire Engineering Sit-ins 101 et seq
Law Commission 129
Lawrence Scott 103
Leadgate Engineering 134
Legal actions 102, 108-9, 120
Leicester Photographic and Litho Service 102, 108
Lennon, John 34
Linder, W. 18
Lindsay, William 71
Linotype 104
Lip 117 Liquidator, UCS 35
Litton Industries 112, 140 et seq
Liverpool Echo 29
Liverpool Free School 68, 133
Locke, J. 155
London Leather Manufacturers' Co-op 15
Lucas 106, 152, 153, 164
Luddism 13
Lyon Group 55, 110

M

MacPherson, C.B. 163, 165
Manchester Billiard Table Makers 15
Mann, Tom 16, 40
Manpower Services Commission 146
Marathon Manufacturing 36, 124
Marx, Karl 98, 125, 154-5
Mat manufacturers, Long Melford 15
Mathew Swain 104
McCormick Screen Printing 107
McGill, Jack 18, 37
McGrath, John 68
McKay and Barr 147
McKee, Ian 55, 56

McLafferty, Eddie 51, 53, 54, 56
Melchett, Lord 77
Meriden 124, 138
Metal Box 104
Metal Mechanics 114
Metra Consulting Group 109, 111, 115, 116
Metra-Weddle Report 90
Militant, the 53
Millan, Bruce 54
Milligan, Arthur 54, 71
Mills, A.J. 111, 112, 116
Ministry of Defence 49
Mirlees Blackstone 103
Mold, Flints 56 et seq
Mooney, Bel 135 et seq, 147
Morning Star 53, 54, 61, 72, 73, 81
Morrison, Herbert 159
Motor unionism, USA 13
Murray, Len 124-5
Murray, Robin 45, 87
Myers, Sir Arthur 57

N

Napiers 29
National Coal Board 135, 149
National Enterprise Board 140
National Industrial Relations Court 108
National Transport Policy 42
Nationalisation 149 et seq
NATKE 114
NATSOPA 114
New Society 76, 82, 103, 116
NGA 114
Nicholson, Brian 42, 48
Nightsbridge Ltd. 134
North East TU Studies Unit 114, 116
Northampton shoe-makers co-op 15
Norton-Villers Triumph 124, 138
NUFLAT 115, 133
NUJ 114
NUPE 114

O

Occupation News (Plesseys) 51, 71
Owen, Robert 14

P

P & O Lines 12

Parkinson-Cowan 63, 66
Parnell, Mike 145
Parsons 79
Parliamentary Labour Party 33
Patternmakers 114
Peel, Jack 113
Pigou, A.C. 91
Pirelli, Aberdare 107
Players 158
Plesseys 49 et seq, 63, 71, 101, 107, 110, 160
Popular Front 13
"Power-pack" 152
Preis, Art 18
Preventative actions by employers 117
Printing industry rationalisation 126
Public services 152

R

Record Electrical 104
Red Mole, the 12, 18, 53, 58, 69, 71, 72
Redundancy 29, 31
Reed, William 136
Reference groups 157
Reid, Jimmy 22, 34, 35, 39
Revisionists 158
Ridley, Nicholas 25
Ridley Report 26
River Don Steelworks 76 et seq, 101
Road-rail car 154
Robens, Lord 11
Rochdale 14
Rolls Royce 21, 157
Rousseau, J.J. 154
Royal Naval Torpedo Factory 50
Royal Navy 49
Ruston Paxman 103

S

Scaffold 68
Scanlon, Hugh 113
Scotsman, the 37, 71
Scotstoun Yard 24
Scott Bader Commonwealth 133
Scott Lithgow 26
Scottish Co-operative Ironworks 14
Selby 149
Serck Heat Transfer 103
Seven Days 59, 62, 72, 73

INDEX

Sexton's 115, 124
Shapiro, Susan 82
Sheffield 76
Sheriden, Geoffrey 82
Sheriff's Act 129
Shipbuilding crisis 23
Shipbuilding Industry Board 2
Shipping services 95
Shore, Peter 139
Sidney, Mr 64
Simon-Vicars 104
SLADE 102, 114, 125
Slater, M 18
Smith, Adam 17
Snow Engineering 101
Social Audit 80, 83 et seq
Socialist Labour League 39, 48
Socialist Worker 48, 53, 72, 112
Solidarity 18, 69
Spina Bifada 153
Spinners 68
Split shipyard 45
Spriano, P. 18
Spriggs, Jack 61, 62, 65, 66, 67, 70, 160
Stanmore Engineering 102
Staples, Tom 60
'Status quo' 41, 125
Stavely Group 104
Stewart, Sir Ian 85
Stibbe & Co. 135 et seq
Stick and Cane Makers' Co-op 15
Strikes 150
Sunday Times 54, 59, 78
Swallow, Sir William 85
Syder, D.G. 108

T

TASS 78, 114, 127
T&GWU 42, 114, 143
Thames Building Co-op 146
Thatcher, M. 150
Thomas Brian, 72
Thompson, W. 37
Thorn Electrical Industries 62, 63, 67
Thorn, Sir Jules 64

Thorneycroft (BLMC) 105, 124
Times, the 54, 62, 71, 72, 81, 96
Tocher, John 105
Tolpuddle Martyrs 14
Town and Country Planning Act 161
Triumph Meriden 76, 124
Tube Investments 107
TUC 123
Twentieth-Century Socialism 158

U

Unemployment, 11, 12, 30, 92, 93, 149 et seq
Upper Clyde Shipbuilders 11, 21 et seq, 80, 87 et seq, 124, 149
Urwin, Harry 127
Uttoxeter 57

V

Vacancies 92
Vale of Belvoir 149
Varley, Eric 140
Viking 104

W

Wadey, Celia 144
Walsall Co-operative Padlock Society 14, 15
Watkins, David 146
Westland Helicopters 12
Wilberforce Enquiry 98
Wilson, Roy 77
Wilson, Sir Harold 60, 64, 68, 140
Wingrove and Rogers 104
Word, the 52, 71
Workers' control 40, 59
Workers' co-operatives 14 et seq, 24, 133 et seq
Workers' Press 53
'Working-days gained' 109

Y

Yarrow, Sir Eric 25
Yarrow's Shipyard 24, 88
Yugoslav self-management 45

Trade Unions in Britain

Ken Coates and Tony Topham

"enormous value . . . fills a major need and deserves to be read throughout the Labour movement and way beyond it . . . detailed and scholarly, presenting all points of view and examining all the relevant literature . . . A mine of useful information, cautious in its judgments and clear in its expression, it will be essential reading for everybody who wishes to appreciate the central importance of unions in the nation's affairs."

Ben Pimlott, *Labour Weekly*

"If you want to know the chronology of the mergers which have produced the trade unions of today, or the detailed functions and working of the Trades Union Congress, or what the Donovan Commission on Trade Unions recommended, or the history of the evolution of national conciliation procedures, or the content of the trade union legislation of the past 15 years, or the trend of strikes over the same period: this is your book."

Metal Mechanics News

"In *Trade Unions in Britain* is all the information which you wanted to know and didn't know where to find, buttressed by 53 statistical tables and written in clear, straightforward prose. It is a best buy, both for its content and because it is cheap for a major book these days."

David Rubinstein, *Labour Leader*

"offers what is now the best introduction to its subject."

John Saville, *Morning Star*

Cloth £14.50   Paper £4.95

Available from Bertrand Russell House, Gamble Street, Nottingham NG7 4ET.